OGLETHORPE COUNTY GEORGIA

Superior Court
Minutes

- *1794-1799* -

(Volume #1)

Compiled by:
Michael A. Ports

Southern Historical Press, Inc.
Greenville, South Carolina

Please direct all correspondence and orders to:

www.southernhistoricalpress.com
or
SOUTHERN HISTORICAL PRESS, Inc.
PO BOX 1267
375 West Broad Street
Greenville, SC   29601
southernhistoricalpress@gmail.com

ISBN #0-89308-838-2

Printed in the United States of America

Introduction

On December 19, 1793, the Georgia General Assembly created Oglethorpe County from a portion of Wilkes County and designated Lexington as the seat of its government. In 1794, a portion of Greene County was added to Oglethorpe, and the boundary between Oglethorpe and Greene shifted several times in 1799. In 1811, Oglethorpe lost territory to the newly formed Madison County. In 1813, Oglethorpe acquired land from Clarke County. Taliaferro County took land from Oglethorpe in 1831, and Oglethorpe received land from Madison County in 1842. The Legislature divided the state into judicial districts, assigning Oglethorpe to the Western Circuit, comprised of Elbert, Franklin, Greene, Hancock, Jackson, Lincoln, and Wilkes counties. The judges, elected to serve three-year terms, held court in each county at least twice per year, as they traveled from county to county within their circuit. The Superior Court had Jurisdiction over all criminal matters, most civil cases, appeals from the Inferior Courts and Justice's Courts, divorces, grand juries, naturalizations, admissions to the bar, and registration of land deeds.

The first volume of Superior Court minutes begins on March 15, 1794 and continues through April 1, 1799. The following transcription was made from the microfilm photographed at the courthouse on November 15, 1957 by the Genealogical Society of Salt Lake City, Utah and is available at the Georgia Archives in Morrow, Georgia and the Family History Library. The heading on the microfilm roll reads

Oglethorpe County Georgia

Superior Court

Minutes

1794 – 1799

On the front cover of the record volume is printed

A

Minutes of first
Superior Court held
in
Oglethopre County

1

The original record volume is not indexed; however, a complete full-name index follows the transcription. The reader should note that a surname appearing in the index without a first name indicates that no first name appears in the minutes, for example Mr. Smith, Smith and Company, Captain Smith, or said Smith. An index entry in the form ___, Jesse indicates that a first name was entered in the minutes, but without any surname, as in Jesse, a free person of color, or the surname is obliterated by a torn page, ink blot, or other imperfection. The clerk entered consecutive numbers at the top of the original pages The numbers in the transcription appearing between brackets, for example [72], signify the original page numbers, entered in the upper right-hand corner of each original page.

Thomas P. Carnes, William Stephens, William Stith, Jr., Benjamin Taliaferro, and George Walton presided as judge during the period covered by the transcription. During the same period, Josiah Cole, William Hay, and John Lumpkin served as court clerk; although, based solely upon the handwriting, five or possibly six others served as deputy clerks. For the most part, their handwriting is legible, making the transcription straightforward and not too difficult. The occassional ink smear or other imperfection is noted within brackets, for example [smear], [torn], or [illegible].

Sometimes the clerks formed the letters "a" and "o" in a very similar manner, making abbreviations such as Jas. and Jos. and sunames Harman and Harmon or Low and Law impossible to distinguish. At other times, the letters "a" and "u" are too similar to differentiate between such names as Burnett and Barnett. The formation of the letters "i" and "e" sometimes makes it difficult to distinguish between such names as Melton and Milton, for example. Also, the clerk formed the capital letters "I" and "J" identically. Determining which letter usually is straightforward when the first letter of a name, but entirely a guess when a middle initial. Sometimes the clerk crossed the letter "t" by extending the horizontal line across the entire word, making it difficult to distinguish between such surnames as Cutter, Cutler, and Culter or Cotton and Colton. Occasionally, the clerk failed to cross the letter "t" at all, leaving the reader wondering if the name was Jewett or Jewell, for example. The transcription follows Sperry's recommended guidelines for reading early American script.[1]

The transcription does not correct any grammar or spelling, no matter how obvious the errors, but does add a few commas, apostrophes, and periods for

---

[1] Sperry, Kip. *Reading Early American Handwriting.* Genealogical Publishing Company, Inc., Baltimore, Maryland, Sixth Printing, 2008.

clarity. Finally, the clerk entered a vertical squiggly line to delineate case citations and other headings, duplicated by the symbol } in the transcription. Careful researchers will consult either the original record or the microfilm copy either to confirm the transcription or formulate alternative interpretations of the clerks' handwriting.

Generally, the transcription maintains the overall format of the minutes, but presents the case citations, jury panels, lists of witnesses, and other court proceedings in a standard and consistent format. The minutes contain numerous original signatures, beyond merely those of the judge and the clerk, including those of many attorneys, individuals filing bonds for appeals and stays of execution, and their securities, as well as those subscribing to various oaths.

To the right of many of the original signatures, the clerk entered the letters L S enclosed by a squiggly line in the form of a circle or oval as follows

That symbol also is not included in the transcription.

The book is dedicated to the memory of the author's numerous Georgia ancestors, although none ever were residents of Oglethorpe County. Many thanks are offered to the kind, patient, and generous staff of the Georgia Archives, for their assistance and suggestions, not only in locating the original records, but in understanding their historical context. Thanks also are offered LaBruce Lucas of the Southern Historical Press for his sage professional advice and counsel. Special thanks are offered to my mother, Ouida J. Ports, who helped instill in me a deep appreciation of American history and genealogy.

Superior Court Minutes

The following Persons were drawn to serve as Grand Jurors at the Next   [1]
Term of the Superior Court in the County of Oglethorpe by his Honor Judge Stith
15ᵗʰ March 1794.

1. John Shields	9. Vines Collier	17. Hugh McCall
2. John Markes	10. John Hill	18. Jeffrey Early
3. Joel Hurt	11. Nathan Ryan	19. John Collier
4. John Lumpkin	12. Robᵗ Beavers	20. Wᵐ Ramsey
5. James Northington	13. Charles Hay	21. Wᵐ Potts
6. Andrew Bell	14. Isaac Collier	22. Robᵗ McCord
7. Presley Thornton	15. Humpʸ Edmondson	23. Jesse Clay
8. John Garrett	16. Richᵈ Goldsby	

The following drawn as Petit Jurors.

1. Thomas Swan	13. Wᵐ Allen	25. Buckⁿ Ledbetter
2. Wᵐ Richards	14. Benʲ Thomas	26. Isham Davis
3. Richᵈ Wright	15. Moses Miligan	27. James Hodges
4. Jesse Coleman	16. Nathan Nall	28. Benʲ Tribble
5. Walter Bell	17. Archelˢ Pope	29. John Holloway
6. Wᵐ James	18. Spencer Thomas	30. Johnson Clarke
7. Robᵗ Galasby	19. [blank]	31. Jnᵒ Wakefield
8. Hugh Roan	20. [blank]	32. Jaˢ Rutlidge
9. John Herring	21. George Taylor	33. Jaˢ Thompson
10. David Thurman	22. Jnᵒ Goldsby, Jʳ	34. Joˢ Bowen
11. Levi Phillips	23. Wᵐ Biers	35. Henry Potts
12. Danˡ McIntosh	24. Challon Scoggons	36. Jesse Starky

Test. Josiah Cole, C. O. C.   W. Stith, junʳ

June Term 1794   [2]

At a Superior Court held at Charles Lain's in and for the County of Oglethorpe
on the 10ᵗʰ of June 1794. Present, his Honor Judge Stith.

William Muire   }
         vs   } Case
Joseph Wheelright }

4

I, Joseph Wheelright, Defendant, & we, John Manor & Robert Beavers, securities, do Acknowledge ourselves indebted to the Plaintiff in the sum Mentioned in the bail bond on this condition, That if the Defendant be cast in this Suit he will pay the Condemnation Money, or surrender himself to the common Goal of this County, or we will do it for him.

Test. Josiah Cole, C.

Grand Jury Sworn

1. John Lumpkin	7. Robert Beavers	13. John Collier
2. John Marks	8. Jeffrey Early	14. Isaac Collier
3. Andrew Bell	9. William Potts	15. John Shields
4. Charles Hay	10. Robert McCord	16. Presley Thornton
5. Richd Goldsby	11. Joel Hurt	17. Hump^y Edmondson
6. John Garrett	12. Jesse Clay	18. Ja^s Northington

Lipham & Moore }   [3]
     vs   } Case
Joseph Wilson }

I do confess Judgment for the sum of eight Pounds & ten pence half penny, with cost, with five Months stay of Execution, to be discharged on the payment of good proof Peach brandy delivered at the Town of Washington, if paid by the time at 4/8 Per Gallon.

Test. Jno Matthews   Joseph Wilson

William Moore, Ass^{ee} }
     vs   } Case
John Shropshire   }

Dismissed at Plaintiff's Cost.

Hugh Freeman   }
     vs   } Ejectment
Alexander Gordon }

On motion of the Plaintiff's Attorney, the Process was ordered to be amended to read Hugh Freeman, Junr.

Hugh Freeman, Junr}

        vs   } Ejectment

Alexander Gordon

On Motion of L. Jones, Attorney for the Plaintiff

Ordered, that a resurvey be had of the Land in dispute between the Parties by the County Surveyor, to be appointed by the Court, and a Surveyor to be appoined by each of the Parties, should they or either of them

Think proper to appoint one, provided fifteen days Notice be given by the   [4] Plaintiff to the Defendant of the time of Making such survey, and it is further ordered that the said County Surveyor do return an Accurate Plat of said Land, shewing the particular manner in which the lines interfere.

Henry Josey   }

        vs   } Covenant

Joseph Wilson & }

Saml Wilson   }

In this Case, the Attorney for the Defendant craved Oyer of the bond upon which the Action was brought.

John Griffin, Attor^y
for Defendant

The Court adjourned till 10 O'Clock tomorrow morning.

W. Stith, jun^r

Wednesday the 11th June 1794

The Court met according to Adjournment. Present, his Honor Judge Stith.

Shadrack Kennebrew   }

        vs   } Case

Martin Nall & Nathan Nall }

Ordered, the Process be amended and a Term given the Defendants.

Michael & Sims }   [5]
     vs   } Case
John Reynolds }

Ordered, that the same be continued.

Abraham Simons }
     vs   } Case
George Lumpkin }

I do confess Judgment for the sum of thirteen Pounds ten shillings and ten pence, with cost and stay of Execution two Months.

George Lumpkin

The State   }
     vs   } Arson
Elijah Pope }

True Bill.   John Lumpkin, fm

The Prisoner, Elijah Pope, was brought into Court and being arraigned, pleaded not Guilty and was ordered into the custody of the Sheriff.

The State   }
     vs   } Indic[t] retailing Spirits
Thomas Hill }

A True Bill.   John Lumpkin, F.

Traverse.

The following Jurors was sworn.

1. Willis Richardson	5. John Holloway	9. Jesse Starky
2. Robert Galasby	6. Levi Phillips	10. Johnson Clarke
3. John Herring	7. Ben[j] Thomas	11. Archelus Pope
4. George Taylor	8. Hugh Roan	12. William Biers

The Jury returned the following verdict, "Guilty."

Ge[o] Taylor, fm

The State }
    vs   } Ind^t retailing Spirituous liquor   [6]
John Stiles }

True Bill.   John Lumpkin, F.

Traverse.

The same Jury sworn as in the case of the State against Thomas Hill, who returned the following Verdict, "Guilty."

                                 Ge^o Taylor, foreman

Phineas Miller   }
    vs   } Case
Joseph Wheelright }

We, John Dimond & Thomas Patton, Securities for the Defendant, in the sum mentioned in the bail bond on these condition that, if the Defendant be cast in this suit he will pay the condemnation money, or surrender himself to the Common Goal of this County, or we will do it for him.

Ack^d in Court
Josiah Cole, C.

The State   }
    vs   } Ind^t selling Liquor without Licence
Celia Waters }

True bill.   John Lumpkin, F.

Traverse.

The same Jury sworn as in the cases of the State againt Thomas Hill & the same vs John Stiles, who return the following verdict, Guilty.

                               George Taylor, Forem

Francis Gordon & Co }
    vs   } Case   [7]
William Rogers   }

I do acknowledge the service of the within Petition and Process, and confess Judgment for the sum of seven Pounds seventeen shillings, with Interest and cost, with stay of Execution till the first of March.

William X Rogers, his Mark

Solomon Loveall }
George McFall }
     vs } Ejectment
Simpleton Spondall }
David Hillhouse }

I acknowledge the service and Notice of the within Declaration.

David Hillhouse

The State }
    vs } Ind^t selling Liquor without Licence
John Hannah }

True Bill.   John Lumpkin, F.

The State }
    vs } Negro Stealing
Charles Cavenah }
& John Sharp }

True Bill.   John Lumpkin, F.

Arraigned and pleaded not Guilty.

The State }   [8]
    vs } Ind^t selling Liquor without licence
Robert Warnack }

True Bill.   John Lumpkin, F.

Richard Bailey }
    vs } Covenant
James Kenny & }
Samuel Patton }

Continued at Defendant's Costs. Cost paid.

John Williamson }
     vs   } Covenant
Joseph Wilson   }

Settled at the Defendant's Cost.

John McDowell }
     vs   } Covenant
James Kenny   }

Continued, Cost paid.

The State }
    vs   } Perjury
James East}

True Bill.   John Lumpkin, F.

Arraigned and pleaded not Guilty.

The State }
    vs   } Forgery
John Hines}

True Bill.   John Lumpkin, F.

Arraigned & pleaded not Guilty.

Richard Royston   }   [9]
      vs   } Case
Joseph Wheelright }

I, Joseph Wheelright, Def^t, and we, Robert Lumpkin& Joseph Eckols, securities, do Acknowledge our selves Indebted in the sum mentioned in the Bail Bond on these conditions, that if the Defendant be cast in this Suit, that he will pay the Condemnation Money, or surrender himself to the Common Goal, or we will do it for him.

Jesse Laine   }
    vs   } Case
Russell Jones }

I, Russell Jones, Def¹, and we, Patton Wise & John Martin, securities, do Acknowledge our selves Indebted to the Plaintiff in the sum Mentioned in the bail bond on these conditions, that if the Defendant be cast in this Suit, that he will pay the Condemnation Money, or surrender himself to the Common Goal of this County, or we will do it for him.

The State   }
    vs   } Deceit
Wᵐ Fletcher   }
Jaˢ Murphy &   }
Wᵐ Shropshire }

A True Bill.   John Lumpkin, foreman

Arraigned & Pleaded not Guilty.

John Ray   }   [10]
    vs   } Case
Henry Garrett }

I, Henry Garrett, Defendant, & Jesse Clay, Security, do Acknowledge our selves Indebted to the Plaintiff in the sum Mentioned in the bail bond on these Conditions, that if the defᵗ be Cast in this suit, he will pay the Condemnation Money, or surrender himself to the Common Goal of this County, or I will do it for him.

Ackᵈ. Josiah Cole, C.

The State   }
    vs   } Indᵗ
Jeremiah Dicken }

No bill.   John Lumpkin, F.

The State   }
    vs   } Indᵗ for deceit
James Murphy }

11

I, James Murphy, & I, Thomas Loyd, do acknowledge our selves Indebted to the State in the Sum of fifty Pounds each Conditioned that, if the said James Murphy Attend the Superior Court this Term from day to day to Answer the above Complaint and not depart the Court without leave.

Ack[d]. Josiah Cole, C.

The State   }   [11]
    vs   } Ind[t] for deceit
William Fletcher }

I, William Fletcher, with John Cargill do Acknowledge our selves Indebted to the State in the Sum of Fifty Pounds each conditioned that, if the said William Fletcher Attend the Superior Court from day to day untill he be discharged by the said Court.

Ack[d]. Josiah Cole, C.

The State   }
    vs   } Ind[t]
William Shropshire }

I, William Shropshire, with Hugh Roan, Security, do acknowledge our selves Indebted to the State of Georgia in the sum of Fifty Pounds each conditioned that, if the said William Shropshire Attend the Superior Court this Term from day to day untill he be discharged by the said Court.

Ack[d]. Josiah Cole, C.

Nathan Nalls, summoned on the Petit Jury, was excused from age.

The State   }   [12]
    vs   } Mis[dn]
Jeremiah Dickens}

No bill.   John Lumpkin, F.

The State   }
    vs   } Larceny
Charles Cavenah }
& John Sharp   }

Charles Cavenah & John Sharp & Jesse Clay & Benjn Greene came into Court and Acknowledged themselves Indebted to his Excellency the Governor and his Successors in Office, the said Charles Cavenah & John Sharp in the sum of Two Hundred Pounds each and the said Jesse Clay & Benjamin Greene in the sum of One hundred Pounds each, to be levied on their lands & Tenements, Goods & Chattels respectively, to be void on condition that the said Charles Cavenah & John Sharp shall Appear in Court Tomorrow Morning at 10 O'Clock to Answer the above Charge and not to depart the Court without leave.

The Court Adjourned till 9 O'Clock tomorrow morning.

W. Stith, jun^r

Thursday 12th June 1794. The Court met According to Adjournment.   [13]
Present, Judge Stith.

The State }
    vs   } Forgery
John Hines }

The Prisoner being brought to the Bar for his trial, the following Jury was elected and sworn (to wit).

1. Wm Richardson	5. Isham Davis	9. Ja^s Thompson
2. Robert Gallaspie	6. John Holloway	10. Jesse Starky
3. John Herring	7. Levi Phillips	11. Benjn Trible
4. Buckner Ledbetter	8. Benjn Thomas	12. Archelus Pope

Who return the following verdict, not Guilty.

Robt Gillespie, forem

Collen Reed }
    vs   } Case
Jeffrey Early }

I, Jeffrey Early, Defendant, & Willm Potts, Security, do Acknowledge our selves Indebted to the Plantiff in the sum mentioned in the Bail Bond on this Condition, that if the defendant should be cast in this suit, he will pay the condemnation

13

Money, or surrender himself to the Common Goal of this County, or I will do it for him.

Ack[d] in Court. Josiah Cole

The State   }   [14]
    vs   } Indictment for Perjury
James East }

The Defendant was brought to the Bar for his trial, the following Jury was elected and sworn, to wit.

1. Robert Galaspie	5. Isham Davis	9. Hugh Roan
2. John Herring	6. John Holloway	10. Jesse Starky
3. George Taylor	7. Levi Phillips	11. Ja[s] Thompson
4. Buckner Ledbetter	8. Benj[n] Thomas	12. Ben[j] Trible

Who return the following Verdict, not Guilty.

Ge[o] Taylor, forem

The State   }
    vs   } Indictment for Horse Stealing
John Claghorn }

True Bill.   John Lumpkin, f.

Arraigned and Pleaded not guilty, and Ordered into Custody of the Sheriff.

The State   }
    vs   } Ind[t] for Negro stealing
Charles Cavenah }
& John Sharp   }

The Prisoners being brought to the bar to be tried, the following Jury was sworn, to wit.

1. Robert Galaspie	5. Isham Davis	9. Hugh Roan
2. Jn[o] Herring	6. John Holloway	10. Jesse Starky
3. George Taylor	7. Levi Phillips	11. James Thompson
4. Buckner Ledbetter	8. Ben[j] Thomas	12. Ben[j] Trible

who say, It is the Opinion of the Jury that Sharp is not Guilty, that Carvenah is guilty of the Charge within.

Ge° Taylor, forem

John Goldsby   }   [15]
     vs   } Casse
James East, Jun[r] }

March 31st 1793. We, Thomas Black, Timothy Carrington, Charles Campbell, Sen[r], & William Strother, with Henry Hill as Umpire, do award that the Legacy, to wit, the Stock of all kinds, the Household furniture, all Debts due and given by Peter Goldsby, Dec[d] to Nancy, his Wife, is the Property of James East, Jun[r], Def[t], at the suit of John Kerby Goldsby, by his Next friend, done at the house of John Smith the day & Year above.

The Hornorable the }   Thomas Black
Superior Court of   }   Timothy Carrington
Oglethorpe County }   Charles Campbell
                                        William Strother
                                        Henry Hill

We, the Grand Jury for the County of Oglethorpe, Make the following Presentments.

We Present as a grievance the neglect of the Commissioners in not assertaining the Center of the County and fixing on a Plan for the Public Building, and as Roads, Bridges, &c appears Properly to come before the Honorable the Inferior Court, and we know not how farr they have taken up the Business, therefore we recommend to the Next Inferior Court to be held for the County to take the Business fully under their consideration, and Appoint Commissioners for laying out and keeping

In repair all Necessary Roads, for the Convenience of the County at large,   [16] as we conceive we cannot do any thing in that business untill the Public Buildings are fixed.

We return our thanks to his Honor the Judge for his Judicious Charge to the Grand Jury and for his Particular attention to the Business of the County.

Given under our hands and seals June Term 1794.

John Lumpkin, F.	Joel Hurt
John Marks	Jesse Clay
Andrew Bell	John Collier
Charles Hay	Isaac Collier
Richd Goldsby	John Shields
John Garrett	Presley Thornton
Jeffrey Early	Humphrey Edmonson
William Potts	James Northington
Robert McCord	

The Court adjourned till tomorrow at 10 O'Clock in the forenoon.

ex^d W. Stith, jun^r

The Court met according to adjournment. Present, his Honor Judge Stith.

The State   }
    vs   } Ind^t house burning
Elijah Pope }

The Prisoner being brought to the bar to be tried, the following Jury was sworn, to wit.

1. Robert Gallasby	5. Thomas Swan	9. Benjn Trible
2. George Taylor	6. Benjn Thomas	10. Arch^s Pope
3. Buckner Ledbetter	7. Jesse Starky	11. Henry Potts
4. John Holloway	8. Ja^s Thompson	12. John Nall

who returned the following Verdict, "we find the Prisoner to be Guilty of the Charge and Recommend him to Mercy."

Ge^o Taylor, F.

Francis Gordon & Co }
    vs   } debt
Duham Demontrony & }
Micajah Williamson   }

By Virtue of a Warrant of Attorney to me directed & Contained in the body of the Bond within declared upon, I do appear for the Defendants in this Case and Acknowledge the service of the within Declaration, and confess Judgment for the sum of Fifty Pounds, with Ineterst from the first day of May 1793.

Jn° Matthews, Att^y
for the Defendants

William Walker, for the }   [18]
use of Fran. Gordon & C°}
      vs   } Case
John Echols   }

I do acknowleddge the Service of this Petition and do confess Judgment for the sum of fifty pounds, with Interest from the 25th of December 1794 and Cost, with stay of Execution untill the first day of January, on Approved Security being as required by Law.

Test. Jn° Matthews   John Echols

If the Defendant doth not give security, Exn° not to Issue for one Month.

Henry Garrett   }
      vs   } Attachment
Thomas Johnson }

On motion of J. Matthews, Attorney for the Plantiff in this Case, ordered the following Property levied by a Writ of Attachment at the suit of said Garrett, as the Property of Thomas Johnson, and not replevied as the law directs, be Sold under the same Regulations as property taken in Execution, and that the Money arising from such Sale be deposited in the Clerk's Office of Oglethorpe County, and that the same be subject to the

Order of the Court, Viz, Two Cows, Two Yearlings, & one Calf, One   [19]
Bed & furniture, one Woman's Saddle, some earthen Ware, 1 looking glass, and one Tea Kettle.

The State   }
      vs   } Horse Stealing
John Claghorn }

The Prisoner being brought to the Bar to be Tried, the following Jury was sworn, to wit.

1. John Herring	5. Thomas Swan	9. John Nall
2. Buck[n] Ledbetter	6. Ben[j] Thomas	10. John Hudging
3. Isham Davis	7. Ja[s] Thompson	11. John Hines
4. John Holloway	8. Henry Potts	12. John Dimond

Who Returned the following Verdict, "We, the Jury, find the Prisoner at the Bar not Guilty."

John Hines, foreman

Thomas Terry   }
     vs   } Attachment
John Rakestraw }

Charles Lane, being summoned in this Case as Garnishee, deposeth and sayeth that at the time the Attachment was levied he had in his Possession a Bond, the Property of said Rakestraw, given to him for Titles by Isham Williams, to part of a Tract of Land granted to Andrew McNab, and conveyed from the said Andrew McNab to John Edwards, Adjoining

Lands belonging Ephraim Pharr & Joseph Wilson, containing Two   [20] Hundred Acres, & that part for which the bond was given in part of said Tract & Contains eighty Acres, more or less, and he further saith that the said bond given to the said Rakestraw by Isham Davis to make titles to Eighty Acres of Land, part of the said Tract containing Two Hundred Acres, more or less, & Granted to the said Andrew, as aforesaid, was taken out of his Possession without his knowledge or Consent.

The following persons were drawn to serve as Grand Jurors at Next term.

1. Henry Hill, 2. Thomas Duke, 3. Hugh Ector, 4. Richard Harvey, 5. Samuel Smith, 6. Tho[s] Hill, 7. William Scott, 8. John Luckie, 9. Humphrey Thompkin, 10. William Walker, 11. James Davenport, 12. Abraham Easter, 13. Joseph Ellsbury, 14. Micajah McGehee, 15. Jacob Carter, 16. Alexander Gordon, 17. Charles Smith, 18. Asa Simmons, 19. Theophilus Ellison, 20. Cha[s] Burk, 21. Joseph Thomas, 22. Thomas Meriwether, 23. Joseph Scott

And the following persons were

drawn to serve as Petit Jurors at the Next Term. [21]

1. Thomas Crane, 2. Danl Saffold, 3. Wm Tate, 4. Jeremiah Fletcher, 5. Matt^w Galloway, 6. Joseph Woodall, 7. John Raine, 8. Middleton Brooks, 9. Jerem^h Dicken, 10. Radford Ellis, 11. Jacob Burton, 12. James Park, 13. Jacob Everhart, 14. John Arnold, Senr, 15. Jo^s Gordon, 16. Lewis Pope, 17. Thos Reynolds, 18. Phillip Scoggin, 19. Joseph Staton, 20. Thomas Norton, 21. James Wilson, 22. Robert Haynes, 23. David Bridges, 24. Russell Jones, 25. Wm Worrell, 26. John Anthony, 27. Thomas Arnold, 28. Stephen Potts, 29. James Sanders, 30. Micajah Clarke, 31. Abraham Zuber 32. John Anderson, 33. Nathan Edwards, 34. Danl Loyd, 35. Nathan Oneal, 36. Edmond Bouchanan

The Court adjourned till tomorrow morning at Nine o'Clock.

W. Stith, jun^r

Saturday 14th June 1794

The Court met according to adjournment. Present, Judge Stith.

The State	}	[22]
vs	} Indictment for Negro Stealing	
Charles Cavenah	}	

The Prisoner being Convicted on an Indictment for Negro Stealing, on Motion of the Attorney General, was broght to the Bar to receive Sentence, and it was demanded of him if he had ought to say why Judgment of Death should not now be pronounced on him, and nothing being said to the Contrary, it is Ordered and adjudged by the Court that the said Charles Cavenah be remanded into the Custody and safe keeping of the Sheriff and there to remain untill the Second day of July next, between the Hours of eleven of the Clock in the forenoon and two of the Clock in the afternoon of the same day, the said Charles Cavenah shall be carried to the Place of Execution and then and there be hanged by the Neck untill he be Dead.

The State	}	
vs	} Indictment Arson	
Elijah Pope	}	

19

The Prisoner, being convicted on an Indictment for the Crime of Arson, on Motion of the Attorney General, was brought to the Bar to Receive sentence, and it was demanded of him

if he had ought to say why Judgment of Death should not now be   [23]
pronounced on him, and nothing being said to the Contrary, it is Ordered and adjudged by the Court that the said Elijah Pope be remanded into the Custody and safe keeping of the Sheriff and there to remain untill the Second day of July next, between the Hours of eleven of the Clock in the forenoon and Two of the Clock in the afternoon of the same day, the said Elijah Pope shall be carried to the Place of Execution and then and there be hanged by the Neck untill he be Dead.

```
The State           }
     vs             }  Indictment Deceit
William Fletcher    }
James Murphey &     }
William Shropshire  }
```

The Defendants being brought to the Bar to be Tried, the following Jury was Sworn, to wit.

1. George Taylor	5. Hugh Roan	9. Arch[s] Pope
2. Robert Galasby	6. Jesse Starky	10. Thomas Swan
3. Henry Potts	7. James Thompson	11. John Holloway
4. Thomas Loyd	8. Isham Davis	12. William Biers

Who return[d] the following verdict, "Shropshire Acquited, Fletcher & Murphy Guilty."

Ge[o] Taylor, F.

Where upon, it is ordered and adjudged by the Court that the said   [24]
William Fletcher and James Murphy be remanded to the Custody and safe keeping of the Sheriff and there to remain untill Monday Next, on which day between the Hours of eleven of the Clock in the forenoon and one of the Clock in the afternoon, he the said William Fletcher shall receive thirty Nine lashes on his bare back at the Public whiping post, and the said James Murphy on the same day and between the same Hours shall Receive twenty lashes on his bare back at the Public whiping post, that they pay the Cost of Prosecution, and be Discharged.

The State }
   vs   } Indictment for retailing spirituous liquors without licence
Thomas Hill }

The said Thomas Hill being found guilty by the Petit Jury,

It is adjudged by the Court that the said Thomas Hill Pay a fine of Ten Pounds, One half for the use of the County, and the other half to the use of Charles Laine, the Prosecutor.

The State }   [25]
   vs   } Indictment for selling Spirituous liquors without licence
John Stiles }

The said John Stiles being found Guilty by the Petit Jury,

It is considered by the Court that the said John Stiles pay the sum of Ten Pounds, One half to the use of the County, and the other to the use of Charles Laine, the Prosecutor.

The State   }
   vs   } Indictment for retailing liquors
Robert Warnack }

Ordered, that a Bench Warrant Issue against the Defentant returnable to Next Term.

The State }
   vs   } same
John Hannah }

Same Order.

The State   }   [26]
   vs   } Arson
Elijah Pope }

In conformity to the request of the Petit Jury, the Prisoner is recommended to the Mercy of his Excellency, the Governor.

The Court then adjourned till Court in Course.

Test. Josiah Cole, C. S. C.   W. Stith, jun[r]

The following persons were drawn to serve as Grand Jurors at Next Term by his Honor Judge Stith, this 13th June 1794.

1. Henry Hill, 2. Thomas Duke, 3. Hugh Ector, 4. Richard Harvie, 5. Samuel Smith, 6. Thomas Hill, 7. William Scott, 8. John Luckie, 9. Humphrey Thompkins, 10. William Walker, 11. James Davenport, 12. Abraham Easter, 13. Joseph Ellsberry, 14. Micajah McGehee, 15. Jacob Carter, 16. Alexander Gordon, 17. Charles Smith, 18. Asa Simmons, 19. Theophilus Ellison, 20. Charles Burk, 21. Joseph Thomas, 22. Thomas Meriwether, 23. Joseph Scott

And the following persons were drawn to serve as Petit Jurors at the Next Term.

1. Thomas Crane, 2. Daniel Saffold, 3. W[m] Tate, 4. Jere[h] Fletcher, 5. Matt[w] Galloway, 6. Joseph Woodall, 7. John Raine, 8. Middleton Brooks, 9. Jere[h] Dicken, 10. Radford Ellis, 11. Jacob Burton, 12. James Park, 13. Jacob Everhart, 14. John Arnold, S[r], 15. Jo[s] Gordon, 16. Lewis Pope, 17. Tho[s] Reynolds, 18. Phillip Scoggin, 19. Jo[s] Staton, 20. Tho[s] Norton, 21. James Wilson, 22. Robert Haynes, 23. David Bridges, 24. Russell Jones, 25. W[m] Worrell, 26. Jn[o] Anthony, 27. Tho[s] Arnold, 28. Step[n] Potts, 29. Ja[s] Sanders, 30. Micajah Clarke, 31. Abraham Zuber 32. John Anderson, 33. Nathan Edwards, 34. Dan[l] Loyd, 35. Nathan Oneal, 36. Edm[d] Bohanan

December Term 1794   [27]

Tuesday the 9th December 1794, being the time for the Superior Court, his Honor the Judge not Attending, the Clerk Opened Court in the usuall form & Adjourned till Court in Course.

Test. Josiah Cole, C.

Georgia   February 11th 1795

The following Persons were drawn to serve as Grand Jurors at the Next Term of the Superior Court to be held for the County of Oglethorpe by Judge Stith.

1. John Garrett, 2. Joseph Catchings, 3. Thomas Nelms, Sen[r], 4. Peachy Bledsoe, 5. Richard Raffity, 6. Humphrey Tompkins, 7. Burrell Pope, 8. Alexander

Gordon, 9. Richard Harvie, 10. Harrison Musgrove, 11. James Marks, 12. Edmund Daniel, 13. John Wilkes, 14. Nathaniel Porter, 15. Thomas Hill, 16. George McFall, 17. William Greene, 18. Micajah Clarke, 19. John Nall, 20. William Streetman, 21. Daniel Goldsby, 22. George Swain, 23. Joseph Parks

And, the following persons were drawn to serve as Petit Jurors at the same Term.

1. Cornelius Carter, 2. Richard Bellamy, 3. John Sorrow, 4. Dunstan   [28] Banks, 5. George Glazner, 6. Charles Sims, 7. William Sharp, 8. Robert Henderson, 9. James McCone, 10. Leonard Young, 11. John Bellamy, 12. Richard Boland, 13. John Cunningham, 14. Edward Riley, 15. William Bryant, 16. William Jones, 17. Jacob Felton, 18. Joel Sims, 19. John Jackson, 20. Nathan Johnson, 21. Samuel Tate, 22. Reubin Phillips, 23. William Battlesby, 24. Charles Hardman, 25. John Shropshire, 26. Josiah Hatcher, 27. Radford Ellis, Jr, 28. Abner James, 29. Seth Stubblefield, 30. Samuel Durham, 31. Cordy Pate, 32. Barnett Smith, 33. Alexander Brown, 34. John Combs, 35. William Lawrance, 36. Nathan Andrews

Attest. Josiah Cole, C.   Ex^d   W. Stith, jun^r

June Term 1795   [29]

At a Superior Court begun and held at the Court house for the County of Oglethorpe on Tuesday the 9th of June 1795. Present, his Honor Judge Walton.

The following persons appeared on the Grand Jury and was were sworn. (to wit)

1. Burrell Pope	7. William Greene	13. Thomas Hill
2. John Garrett	8. Daniel Goldsby	14. John Nall
3. Joseph Catchings	9. Joseph Parks	15. Peachey Bledsoe
4. Thomas Nelms	10. Richd Raffity	16. George Swain
5. Hump^y Tompkins	11. Wm Streetman	17. Alexander Gordon
6. Nathaniel Porter	12. John Wilkes	

Micajah Clarke, being summoned on the Grand Jury, excused.

Collen Reed & C° }
   vs   } Case
Jeffrey Early   }

Setled.

Daniel Burford   }
          vs   }   Ass^t & Batt^y
James Haughton   }

Discontinued.

John Ray, for the use }   [30]
of William Moore   }
          vs   }   Case
Henry Garrett   }

Dismis^d at Defendant's Costs.

William Muire   }
          vs   }   Case
Joseph Wheelwright }
& Isa Carter   }

Abated as to Wheelwright and Non est as to Carter.

Paul Patrack }
      vs   }   Case
John King   }

Jury Sworn, to wit.

1. Alexander Brown   5. John Sorrow   9. Barnett Smith
2. Samuel Durham   6. Samuel Tate   10. Edward Riley
3. Leonard Young   7. John Bellamy   11. Richard Boland
4. John Shropshire   8. Abner James   12. Radford Ellis

We find for the Plantiff the sum of Eight pounds eight Shillings, with Interest
from the Twenty fifth day of December 1793.

John Shropshire, F.

M^r B The Plantiff stays Execution till 25th Decr Next.

John Matthews

24

Duham Demontrony }   [31]
    vs   } Case
Jeffrey Early   }

I do confess Judgment for the sum of Seven Pounds three shillings & eight Pence one farthing, with Cost of Suit, stay of Execution five Months.

                                Jeffrey Early

Thomas Terry }
    vs   } Attach^t
John Rakestraw }

Settled.

Michael & Sims }
    vs   } Case
John Reynolds }

The same Jury as in the case of Paul Patrack vs John King, who returned the following Verdict. We, the Jury, find for the Plantiff the sum of Twelve pounds Nineteen shillings & five Pence, with Interest from the eleventh day of May in the Year 1792, & Cost.

                                John Shropshire, F.

John K. Goolsby }
    vs   } Case
James East   }

Judgment on the award.

Thomas Cooper }   [32]
    vs   } Debt
Nathl Durkie }

Witness for plff Sworn.

John C. Walton, Esqr

By Virtue of a power of Attorney to me directed and herewith filed, I do appear for Nathaniel Durkie, the Def^t, and Receive Declaration & confess Judgm^t to Thomas Cooper, the Plantiff, for the Sum of fifty pounds, with Stay of Ex^n three Months, with Interest & cost of Suit.

John C. Walton

John H. Foster }
       vs   } Sland^r
Jeffrey Early   }

Dis^t at Defendant's Cost.

Thomas Daniel   }
       vs   } Case
Joseph Huntington }
& Elihu Lamar   }

Abated.

Richard Rayston   }
       vs   } Case
Joseph Wheelwright }

Abated.

Russel Jones }
       vs   } Slander
James East   }

Discontinued, Cost paid.

Phenias Miller   }
       vs   } Case
Joseph Wheelwright }

Abated.

Francis Gordon   }
       vs   } Case
Edmond Taylor   }

Setled.

John Martin, Ass^{ee} }   [33]
  vs   } Debt
Elijah Clarke & }
Jeffrey Early }

Discontinued.

Henry Trent }
  vs } Cov^t
Charles Finch }

Abated.

Ge^o Walton

The Court adjourned till Tomorrow morning 9 O'Clock.

Wednesday the 10th 1795

The Court met according to adjournment. Present, his Honor Judge Walton.

Jeremiah Russel }
  vs } Trover
Thomas Duke }

Dismis^d.

William Thompson }
  vs   } Case
Alex^r Gordon }

Continued by Consent.

Richard Copland }
  vs   } Cov^t
Randolph Ramsey }

Continued.

Thomas Simonton }
      vs   } Debt
William Potts   }

Continued.

John Wilson   }
      vs   } Debt
Presley Thornton }

Continued.

Shadrick Kennebrew }
      vs   } Case
Martin Nall &   }
Nathan Nall   }

Continued as to Nathan, And Non Est as to Martin.

John McDowell }   [34]
      vs   } Covenant
James Kenney }

Setled.

David Hilhouse }
      vs   } Petition & Process
Edmond Taylor }

Continued.

Peter Cartwright }
      vs   } Slander
Eps Tatom   }

Cont[d] by Affidavit.

Thomas Gibbons, Esq[r] }
      vs   } Debt
Andrew Hawk   }

Jury Sworn, to wit.

Alex^r Brown	Barnet Smith
Saml Durham	Radford Ellis
Leonard Young	John Shropshire
John Sorrow	John Combs
Saml Tate	Seth Stubblefield
Edward Riley	Zaddock Barnett

who Returned the following Verdict. We find for the Plaintiff the Sum of Twenty four Pounds eleven Shillings & five pence, with Interest from the 12th Octr 1790 & Cost.

John Shropshire, forem

The plaintiff gives thirty days for the defd^t to Appeal.

The State }
  vs   } Ind^t Retailing Spirituous Liquors
John Hannah }

Arraign^d & plead^d not Guilty.

Traverse. The same Jury as in the Case of Thomas Gibbons, Esqr vs Andrew Hawk, who Return the following Verdict, "not Guilty."

John Shropshire, foreman

John Doe, on the demise}   [35]
of Hugh Freeman   }
    vs   } Ejec^t
Alex^r Gordon &   }
Richd Roe   }

Cont^d by Affd^t.

Jeffrey Early }
   vs   } fi fa
John Blanton}

Cont^d by Affd^t.

29

Comm^s of the Academy }
and Town of Washington }
       vs } fi fa
James Hart & }
Thomas McCone }

Cont^d by Affd^t.

Henry Trent }
    vs } Case
William Langham }

Cont^d by Consent.

James Goolsby, for the }
Use of John Harris }
     vs } Covenant
Asa Simmons and }
John Griffith }

I do confess Judgm^t for the sum of Thirty three pounds twelve Shillings, with Interest from the Twenty fifth day of Decr 1793. One Thousand seven hundred & Ninety-three, with Stay of Execution till the first Day of Decr Next.

Asa Simmons

Adam Simonton, Adm^r }
of Marg^t Simonton, Dec^d }
     vs } Case
Thomas Simonton, Adm^r }
of Robt Simonton, Dec^d }

The Same Jury as in the Case of Thomas Gibbons ags^t Andrew Hawk & [36] the State vs John Hannah, who Return^d the following Verdict. "We find for the Defd^t."

J. Shropshire, F.

Richard Bailey, Special bail for John Park, at Suit of Trent, ~~Park~~ Delivered Up the said Park, & John Stewart & Jeffrey Earley became Special bail in his Stead.

John Thurmon }
      vs   } Cov^t
Thomas Black }

The same Jury as in the Case of Thomas Gibbons vs Andrew Hawk, who Return the following Verdict. "We find for the plaintiff the Sum of Two hundred & Sixty Seven Dollars & fifty Cents, which may be discharged by the payment of Eight Thousand Nine hundred & Sixty Weight Neet Augusta Inspected Crop Tobacco, with Interest & Cost, Stay of levy five Months by Consent of parties.

John Shropshire, F.

Henry Trent }
      vs   } Case
John Parks }

I do hereby Confess Judgm^t for the Sum of Sixty Dollars, with Interest from the Twenty fifth day of Decr 1792 and Cost, with Stay of Exe^n Untill the first day of January 1796.

John Parks

Mary Cochran }   [37]
      vs   } Case
Edwd Harrison }

Discont^d.

Jesse Lain }
      vs   } Case
Russel Jones }

I do confess Judgment for the Sum of ten pounds Nine Shillings & Six pence, with Stay of Ex^n till the Thirtieth Day of November.

Russe Jones

James Shepperd }
      vs   } Case
Jno Moore &   }
Ge^o Barber   }

Cont^d by Affd^t.

The State }
    vs   } Ind^t for Perjury
Joshua Jennings }

No Bill.   Burr^l Pope, F.

Henry Josey }
    vs   } Cov^t
Joseph Wilson }

Cont^d.

Reubin Goings }
    vs   } Assl^t & Bat^y
Thomas Holland }

~~Cont^d~~ Setl^d.

John Lindsay }
    vs   } Debt
Charles Burk }

Dismised.

Richard Smith, Ass^ee   }   [38]
Zacharias & Salley Colley }
    vs   } Ejmn^t
John Bridges & }
William Stiles }

The same Jury as in the Case of Thomas Gibbons vs Andrew Hawk, who Return the following Verdict. upon Motion of Mr Jones, it is Ordered that Berry, Jones, Baines, Merett, Nancy, & Jesse Bridges, Minors & Heirs of David Bridges, be Admited to Defend &c Upon the Usual Rule, by Nathaniel Bridges, their Guardian.

Jurior withdrawn & Cause Discontinued.

Richard Smith, ex dem }
Henry D. Downs   }
        vs   } Eject
William Stiles, tenant in }
Possession Hen^y Reid   }

Upon Motion of Mr Jones, it is Ordered that William Hill be Admited to Defend &c Upon Usual Rule.

Richard Bailey   }
        vs   } Cov^t
James Kenney & }
Saml Patton   }

Cont^d By Affd^t.

James McCammon }
& William McCree }
        vs   } Case
John Wilkins   }

I do Confess Judgment for the Sum of Eight Pounds five Shillings & Nine pence, by Virtue of Authority given & Contained in the Body

of the Note Declared Upon and do also Acknowledge the Service of this   [39] Writ.

> Mathews, Att^y
> for the Deffd^t

Alex^r McCree give evidence as to the truth of the Note.

The following Persons are Drawn to Serve on the Grand Jury the ensuing Term.

1. Thomas Tuggle	9. Jiles Lee	17. James Daniel
2. William Graves	10. Benj^a Blake	18. John Nichols
3. Phillip Ray	11. Joseph Mourton	19. Mark Phillips
4. John Luckie	12. Josiah Jordan	20. Adam Simmons
5. John Bailey	13. Jesse Lacy	21. Elisha Hunter
6. William Mathews	14. John Cargill	22. Thomas Hill

33

7. Joel Hurt	15. Jeffrey Early	23. Wm Harvie
8. Howel Tatum	16. Jn° Lumpkin	

Petit Jury

1. Henry Ramsey	13. Wm Langham	25. William Sorrow
2. John Dunstan	14. Thomas Moody	26. Eps Tatum
3. Samuel Patton	15. Jesse Lee	27. Edwd Bohannan
4. Jeremiah Bogges	16. John McCord	28. David McNalley
5. John Hardin	17. Benj^a Watkins	29. Benj^a Standiford
6. John Stewart	18. Henry Radford	30. Jonathan Bridges
7. David Herring	19. John Vickars	31. Zach^h Arnold
8. John N. Anderson	20. Ja^s Armstrong	32. George Scroggin
9. John Cole	21. Patrick Shields	33. Reubin Radford
10. George Smith	22. Wm Biars	34. Moses White
11. Phillip Edmonson	23. James McGeehe	35. Parks Chandler
12. Henry Hayns	24. Barton Martin	

Richard Smith, ex dem }   [40]
John Blanton   }
     vs   } Eject
William Stiles, tenant in }
Poss^on William Meritt }

Upon Motion of Mr Griffin, it is ordered that William Merritt be admited to defend &c Upon the Usual Rule.

The State   }
    vs   } Ind^t forgery
John Callier }

True Bill.   Burr^l Pope, Fm

The Grand Jury brought in their Presentments, which were Ordered to be published together with the Charge, and also that the presentments Respecting the Retailing of Spirituous liquors without licens be turned into an Indictment next Term.

Ordered also that the Charge and presentments be entered of Record in the Court Books.

Ge° Walton

Gentlemen of the Grand Jury,

It is with more than common Pleasure that I have met You to hold a Court in the County of Oglethorpe, a Name deservedly Respected in a State which was Setled by himself, and one which has populated equal to the possesing through a Revolution and becoming a Member of a great & flourishing Empire within the life of the first Setler, a progress so Rapid and the prospect before Us as extensive and promising Should Opperate Upon the Minds of all good Men

as a Stimulus to effectuate Exertions to Support good Government   [41] by a Prompt Obedience to the laws and the discouragement of all Practices Subversive of Order and the Moral Duties.

To Assist in doing these, the Constitution and the laws have Selected the Grand Inquest twice a Year that breaches of the peace in every Degree and which Comprehend every infraction of the Publick law May be prevented and put in the way of Trial and Punishment in Discharging Your part of this duty. You will with, as Your Oath directs You, divert Yourselves as far as may be of the frailities of human Nature, and Act without favor, affection, or partiality on the one side, or of fear, hatred, or Malice on the other, and Still More without any hope of Reward from any Quarter, whilst we ought not to Spare our friend from attachments, we Should Deter ourselves to let the bad man Escape through fear or any other Consideration on this ground. I am thus emphalie because a Criminal Circulation of false papers of Different & Discriptions and the Signs of Property in different ways, is said to be prevalent, which Opperates, if true, a breach of the laws, an injury to the fair Dealer, and disgrace to the States. Should any thing of this Sort come to Your knowledge, I have no doubt You will Present it, and Should that be the Case You may rely Upon the Strict Execution of the law on the part of the Court.

Gentlemen,

Since my coming into the County, I have learned that Uneasinesses exist among the Citizens on account

35

of the Permanent position of the Court house and Joal. This is to be [42]
lamented, as it may tend to delay the erection of proper & Convenient houses,
indeed the State is not with out instances of Much Expence & inconvenience
experienced upon Similar grounds. The Clause in the Act for fixing upon a place
for the Courthouse and Jaol in this County is Coupled with that for Warren. In
the latter, the latter the Commissioners are Directed to fix it as Nearly Central as
Convenient, and as the Commissioners for this County are appointed in the same
Clause to fix upon a proper place, it ought to be Concluded, that it was intended
it Should be Upon the Same principal as the other, that is, not Necessarily to be
on the Central Point, for that might be on an inconvenient Spot, but to be on most
eligible and Accessible ground some where Near the Center. Never having been
in Your County before, Gentlemen, it is not possible for me to know where that
Spot is, and although the present place appears favourable, it is not for me to
interfere. I have only Mentioned the Subject to Engage Your attention and
Cander. it is a County Matter & as such Merits Your impartial Observation as
Jurors upon Your Oaths and as Citizens who's permanent are Concerned when
ever it may be my wish is for the General Convenience.

Ge° Walton
9th June 1795

Georgia, Oglethorpe County 12th June 1795

We, the Grand Jury for the County aforesaid, on our Oaths, do make the following
presentments, Viz. 1st We feel ourselves agrieved by the Transactions of our last
Legislature Respecting the Sale of our Western Territory & recommend that our
Next Legislature do

take the same into their Serious Consideration and Persue Such [43]
Measures as in their wisdom may Deem propper and Expedient to Support their
Injured Country's Rights.

2nd We Present as a Greviance that the Code of Laws of this State are not so
disfusively Circulated so that Each Civil Officer may be duly furnished with a
copy thereof.

3rd We Present as a Greviance that Our Majistrates do not Use their utmost
Endeavours to Suppress Licencious Practices, Such as Swearing, Gameing,
Drunkeness, Fighting, profaining the Lord's Day &c.

4th We Recommend that our Several Majistrates for this County do meet at this place on the 4th day of July to Consult with Each other and adopt an Uniform Mode of Carrying the laws of this State into due Effect, as fas as Respects the Several Duites of Inferior Majistrates.

5th We present Joseph Wilson for Retailing Spirituous Liquours without Lawful Licens.

6th And lastly, We return our thanks to his Honor the Judge for the Excellent Charge Delivered to us at the Commencement of this Term, and do Recommend that the together with our presentments be published in the State Gazette.

Burrl Pope, Fm	William Streetman	Humphrey Tompkins
George Swain	Peechy Bledsoe	John Wilks
Thomas Nelms	Thomas Hill	Nathaniel Porter
John Garrett	Richd Raffety	Alexander Gordon
William Green	John Nall	Joseph Parks
Joseph Catching	Daniel Goolsby	

The Court Adjourned till Court in Course.

Test. Josiah Cole, C.

December Term 1795   [44]

At a Superior Court begun and held at the Courthouse for the County of Oglethorpe on Tuesday the 8th day of Decr 1795. Present, his Honor Judge Stith.

The following persons appeared on the Grand Jury (to wit).

1. William Graves	5. Benja Blake	9. William Mathews
2. Phillip Ray	6. John Cargile	10. Jeffrey Earley
3. Joel Hurt	7. John Lumkin	11. Joseph Mourton
4. Howel Tatum	8. Mark Phillip	

Benja Blake,, being Sumond on the Grand Jury is Excused.

The Court Adjourned till Tomorr 10 O'clock.

Exd   W. Stith, junr

Wednesday 9th Dec[r] 1795

The Court met According to adjournment. Present, his Honor Judge Stith.

The following persons appeared on the Grand Jury.

1. William Mathews	7. Mark Phillips	13. Will[m] McElroy
2. Joel Hurt	8. John Parks	14. John Shropshire
3. Josep Mourton	9. John McWherter	15. William Graves
4. Jeffrey Early	10. Edm[d] Alexander	16. Phi[l] Ray
5. John Lumkin	11. Hugh Ector	17. John Cargile
6. Josiah Jordan	12. George Cowen	18. Howel Tatum

The Grand Jury, after being Impanneled Returned and and Chose Jeffrey Earley Foreman.

Randolph Ramsey, Resp[t] }
      vs   } Appeal
Rich[d] Copland, app[t]   }

Judgment by Confession

Under Proclamation Judgment Confessed for the Sum of forty two Dollars and Cost, which was not paid at Appealing. Stay of levy till the last day of March Next.

Rich[d] Copland

Isaac Ramsey proved his Attendance as a Witness in This Case. See   [45]
his Account filed in the Process.

The following persons appear on the Petit Jury.

1. Ferdenando Phiniry	7. Jesse Lee	13. Benj[a] Standaford
2. Jeremiah Boggus	8. Reubin Radford	14. Parks Chandler
3. John Cole	9. Patrick Shields	15. Henry Hayns
4. John Leget	10. William Sorrow	16. John Hines
5. George Smith	11. Eps Tatum	17. Thomas Carter
6. Humphrey Edmono[n]	12. Edm[d] Bohannan	

Henry Josse   }
     vs   } Covenant
Joseph & Saml Wilson }

The following Jury Sworn.

1. Ferdinan Phiniry	5, George Smith	9. Eps Tatum
2. Jeremiah Bogges	6. Hump^y Edmonson	10. Edm^d Bohannan
3. John Cole	7. Jesse Lee	11. Benj^a Standaford
4. John Leget	8. Reubin Radford	12. Patrick Shields

We, the Jury, find that the Defendant pay Cost.

Ferdinando Phiniry, fore M^n

David Hilhouse }
     vs   } Case
Edmond Taylor }

Same Jury as above.

We, the Jury, find the Plantiff Recover 25 Dollars 72 Ct^s, with Interest & Cost.

Ferdin^d Phiniry, F. man

Richd Bailey   }
     vs   } Cov^t
James Kenney }
and Saml Patton }

The following Jury Sworn.

1. John Hines	5. Burwell Bruer	9. Henry Ramsey
2. Henry Hayns	6. James Hines	10. David Greer
3. Parks Chandler	7. Thomas Carter	11. John Malone
4. Robert Gresham	8. Isaac Pennington	12. John Hawkins

Return the following Verdict.   [46]

We find for the Plantiff the Sum of Ninety six Dollars, with Cost.

John Hines, F. man

The State   }
     vs   } Ind^t forgery
John Callier }

The said John Callier, being three times Solemnly Called & failed to appear &
Harrison Musgrove being also Called and failing to produce the body of said John
Callier, Ordered that the Recognizance of the said John & Harrison, his Security,
be Estreated & that a Scire Facias Issue against them Returnable to the Next Term
to Shew Cause, if any they have, why Judgment Should Not be Enter^d against
them for the amount thereof.

The Grand Jury for the County Returned the following presentments.

We Return his Honor the Judge our most Respectful thanks for his Judicious
Charge & his Strict Observance to the Law & for his due attendance to business
&c.

We proceed to make the following presentments.

We, the Grand Jury for the County aforesaid, upon Our Oaths, present as a
Greviance and an Injury to this County that the Courthouse & Jaol are not
Established at this place because Conceive it to be the wish of the large Majority
of the good Citizens of the County and the Most Convenient and advantagious

Place to be found at or near the Center of the County for that purpose,   [47]
it being within our knowledge that a General Report & belief hath prevailed that
No Court Could be held during the present Term for this County.

We Recommend that the Court be Adjourned without Entering further Upon the
business of the Term. We are the More Induced to this Opinion from belief that
a Number of the Suiters & Witnesses do not Attend and that a New Arrangement
will take place for the time of holding Courts by the Next Legislature, & we
further Recommend that these, our presentments, be published in the State Gazette
and laid before the Next Legislature.

1. Jeffrey Early, foreman
2. Wm Mathews   7. John Parks   12. W^m McElroy
3. Joseph Mourton   8. Jno McWherter   13. Jno Shropshire
4. Jno Lumpkin   9. Edm^d Alexander   14. Phillip Ray
5. Josiah Jordan   10. Hugh Ector   15. Jno Cargile
6. Mark Phillips   11. George Cowen   16. Howel Tatum

Ordered, that that the foregoing presentments be published According to the Request of the Grand Jury.

A Petition from Peter Early Requesting to be admitted as an attorney in the Several Courts of Law and Equity within this State was presented, and he having Undergone an Examination and being found duly Qualified.

Ordered, that he, the said Peter Early, Esqr, be admited & Enroled as an Attorney in the Several Courts of Law within this State and that his Admission be Recorded.

Joseph Wilson }   [48]
        vs   } Case
John Moore   }

9th Decr 1795

By Virtue of a Power of Attorney to me Directed & herewith filed, I do appear for the Defendant, John Moore, Rec^d Declaration Waiving all errors and Confess a Judgment to Joseph Wilson Thirty Eight pounds Eleven Shillings and Nine pence Sterling and Cost.

Jno Walton, Att^y
for Moore

In Conformity to the Request & Recommendation of the Grand Jury, the Court Adjourned till Court in Course.

Test. W. Hay, Clk   Ex^d W. Stith, jun^r

March Term 1796   [49]

His Honour, Judge Taliaferro, Appeard, Produced his Commission, and Took his Seat as a Judge of the Superior Court.

The Attorney Genl, Peter V. Allin, Esqr, Produced his Commission Also.

After which Harrison Musgrove produced in Oppen Court the Body of John Callier in Discharge of his Bail, Who was Received and the Said Musgrove Discharged.

41

The State   }
     vs   } Indictment
John Callier }

John Lindsey, of the County of Wilkes, And John Parks, of Oglethorpe County,
Came into Court and Acknowledged themselves bound in the Sum of fifty pounds
each to his Excellency the Governor. And the said John Callier in the sum of One
hundred pounds, to be Levied on the goods And Chattels, lands And Tenements
for the personal Appearance of the Said John Callier at the Next Superior Court
of this County, Then and there to Abide the Order of Said Court and Not to depart
the Said Court unless leave given by the Said Court and this Recognizance to be
Void, or else to remain in full force & Virtue.

                                        John Lindsey
                                        John Parks
                                        John Callier

The Court then Adjourned till Court in Course.

W. Hay, Clk   Ben Taliaferro

The following persons were drawn to Serve as Jurors at the Next Term   [50]
of the Superior Court in the County of Oglethorpe By his Honor Judge Taliaferro.
9th of May 1796

                          Grand Jurors

James Marks	Henry Haynes	Thomas Watts
Thomas Hill	John Sankey	John Callier
John Dunn	John Haynes	Edmond Daniel
Thomas Gilmer	John Andrews	John Gresham
William Potts	Thomas Black	John Haynes
William Bledsoe	John Milner	James Parks
Benj Taylor	Abner Biddle	Daniel Roberts
Thomas Merriweather	Richard Hartsfield	John Mathews
Joel Barnett	Thomas Thornton	John Stewart
Absolum Biddle	William Strawther	Josiah Jorden
Frans Meriweather	Elisha Hunter	Alax Gordon 33

Pettit Jurors

Charles McDannel

John Tillery	Barnard Smith	William Jennings
Richard Boland	Ge° Elliot	James Thweat
James Taylor	Sam¹ Hollaway	Zadock Barnard
William Johnson	Abra Zuber	William Ray
John Vickers	Soloman Burford	Michael Wright
Abel Gower	William Sharp	James Kenney
Robert Jennens	John Tarver	Thomas Moodey
Robert Russell	Dorias Brag	John Haynes
John Hail	Ephraim Pharr	Arch Hodge
Joel Simms	David Weaver	Thomas Edmonson
Smith Gaummon	Needham Noris	Paschal Traylor
Sam¹ Shannon	Charles Finch	Nathan Howell
James Cowin	William Brown	Charles Rich
John Jackson	Reubin Mcelrory	John Herring
John Callahan	Joseph Embrey	Edmond Edwards
Jeremiah Dickins	John Laffity	Thomas Maxwell
Edward Greysham	Joseph Grag	Theoˢ Hill
William Easter	James Smith	William Hodge
John Embrey	John Hubbard	John Holaway
William Allin	James East	60

Test. W. Hay, Clk

September Term 1796   [51]

At A Superior Court Held in and for the County of Oglethorpe on the 28th day of September 1796. Present, His Honor Judge Taliaferro.

Grand Jury Sworn

1. John Stewart, Foreman

2. John Dunn	9. William Strawther	16. James Stovall
3. Thomas Gilner	10. James Parks	17. William Walker
4. William Potts	11. William Bledsoe	18. Thomas Dun
5. Thoˢ Meriweather	12. John Smith	19. John Fenning
6. Joel Barnett	13. William Pace	20. Thomas Loyd
7. John Milner	14. Samuel Colquitt	21. Charles Smith
8. Rich Hartsfield	15. John Peacock	

43

Upon Motion of the Solicitor Gen¹.

Ordered, that the Sheriff fourthwith Apply to the Sheriff of Wilkes County for John Sellers, a prisoner confined in the Common Goal of Wilkes County and that Said Sheriff of Wilkes be directed without delay to Deliver the Said John Sellers to the Said Sheriff of Oglethorpe.

James McCaurmon   }
       vs   }
Shropshire & Shropshire }

Abated by Death of the Plaintiff.

Thoˢ Ellerson   }
      vs   }
William Merrett }

I Confess a Judgment for the Sum of Seventy Dollars and Cost of Suit, with Stay of Execution five Months.

Wᵐ Merrett
28ᵗʰ of September 1796

Stephen Williamson }   [52]
      vs   }
Benjamin Edward }

Death of the Defendant Sugested in the usual form.

William Johnson }
     vs   } Debt
John W. Burnes }

Joseph Staton and Robert Jinnings Came into Court & entered themselves Special Bail in the Above Case Agreeable to Law.

James Callier }
   vs   }
John Callier }

Jurors Sworn

1. David Weaver	5. William Brown	9. John Jackson
2. Micael Right	6. Arch Hodge	10. John Herring
3. James Keaney	7. Charles Rich	11. John Hollaway
4. Thomas Moody	8. Pascal Traylor	12. Wm East

Is The Jury Who Returns the following Verdict. We, the Jury, do find for the Plaintiff the Sum of Two Thousand and Ninety four Dollars, With interest & Cost of Suit.

Ja^s Kenney, Forman

James Stallings }
     vs   }   Case
Archer Norris }

I, the Defendant, & we, William Norris & Hardy Norris, Acknowledge Ourselves Jointly and Severally bound to the Plaintiff in the Sum mentioned in the bail Bond on this Condition, that if the Defendant Shall be Cast in this Suit, we will pay the Condemnation money, or Surrender himself as the law directs, or we will do it for him. Taken and Acknowledged in Open Court.

Test. W. Hay, Clk   Wm Norris
                                   Hardy Norris

James Sheapherd }   [53]
     vs   }
John Moore &   }
Ge^o Barber   }

Dismised at the Mutual Costs of Plaintiff & Defendant.

The Court then Adjourned till Ten o'clock Tomorrow morning.

Ben Taliaferro

Thursday the 29th of September 1796

Court Met According to Adjournment. Present, Judge Taliaferro.

The State }
   vs } Indictment Forgery
John Smith }

True Bill.   John Stewart, F. man

The State }
   vs } Indictment Forgery
Elias Hines }

True Bill.   John Stewart, F. man

Kenney & Patton }
   vs } Fifas Returned for Illegallitys
Richard Bayley }

Upon the Application of James Kenney & Saml Patton, Adjudged that the Said Fifas Fas is Illegal and Ordered that the Clerk do Now enter up an Appeal on the Verdict found Against them at the Suit of Richard Bayley in the Court and that the Security for the Same be Now Taken on Other Cases of Appeal.

Henry McElrory }
   vs }
Henry Hill }

Claim Set a Side And Execution Ordered to Issue.

John Griffin &   }   [54]
Thomas Goodwin, Adm^{rs} }
   vs } Trover
James Brooks   }

I, the Defendant, and we, Pascel Traylor & Allen Spurlock, Acknowledge Ourselves Jointly & Severally Bound to the Plaintiff in the Sum mentioned in the Bail Bond, on the Condition that, if the Defendant Shall be Cast in this Suit, we Will pay the Eventual Condemnation money, or Surrender himself as the Law Directs, or we Will do it for him. Taken And Accknowledged in Open Court.

Test. W. Hay, Clk   Pas^l Traylor
                                                    Allen Spurlock

46

John [blank] }
   vs   }
Martin Nall }

Claim Set Aside & Execution Ordered to Issue.

Thomas Gibbons }
   vs   } Sheriff's Report
Andrew Hawk }

Claim of Property by Peter Hawk.

Jury Sworn

1. Richard Boland	5. Solomon Burford	9. James Kenny
2. Wm Johnson	6. John Jackson	10. Pascal Traylor
3. James Cowin	7. Michael Wright	11. John Tarver
4. Abraham Zuber	8. Abel Gower	12. Radford Ellis

Who Returned the following Verdict. We, the Jury, find the Property to be the property of Peter Hawk.

John Tarver, F. man

William Hay & the   }
Heirs of Walton, Dec^d }
    vs   }
The Commissioners of }
The Academy & Town }
of Washington   }

Levies Withdrawn as to Hay. Claim to the Land.

Jeffrey Early }   [55]
   vs   }
John Parks }

Jury Sworn.

1. Obediah Belcher	5. Edmond Alaxander	9. Ge^o Varner
2. Jacob Carter	6. Joshua Tillery	10. Jno Holaway

3. Mathew Stone	7. Geᵒ Hambleton	11. Samˡ Shannon
4. Zadock Barnet	8. William Ealey	12. David McCord

Is the Jury Who Return the Following Verdict. We, the Jury, find for the Plaintiff Two hundred Dollars, With Interest & Cost.

Mathew Stone, F. man

Hugh Freman }
    vs   } Ejectment
Alex Gordon }

The Same Jury as in the Case of Thomas Gibbons vs Andrew Hawk. We, the Jury, do agree that All the Land Within the Original lines Granted to Galaspey is Freman's.

John Tarver, F. man

Elisha Brown & }
Lemuel Black   }
    vs   } Debt
Aventon McElroy }

The Defendant and We, William Bohannon & Billey McElroy, Acknowledge Ourselves Jointly And Severally bound to the Plaintiff in the Sum mentioned in the Bail Bond, on the Condition that, if the Defendant Shall be Cast in this Suit, we will pay the condemnation money, or Surrender himself as the law Directs, or we will do it for him.

Taken And Acknowledged }   Aventon A McElrory, his mark
in Open Court   }   Billey McElrory
                         William A Bohannon, his mark

The Grand Jury Returned The Following Bills.   [56]

The State   }
    vs   } Indictment Horse Stealing
John Sellers }

True Bill.   John Stewart, F. man

The State   }
    vs   } Indictment Assault
William Johnson }

No Bill.   John Stewart, F. man

The State   }
    vs   } Indictment Assault
William Johnson }

No Bill.   John Stewart, F. man

The State   }
    vs   } Indictment Assault
William Johnson }

No Bill.   John Stewart, F. man

Peter Cartright }
    vs   } Slander
Epps Tatum   }

Jury Sworn

1. Obediah Belcher   5. Edmond Alaxander   9. Jn° Holaway
2. Jacob Carter   6. Joshua Tillery   10. Saml Shanon
3. Mathew Stone   7. Ge° Hambleton   11. David McCord
4. Zadock Barnet   8. William Ealy   12. James Cragg

We, The Jury, find for the Plaintiff Two hundred Dollars, With Cost of Suit.

                                            Mathew Stone, F. man

The State   }
    vs   } Indictment Larcenney
William Jones & }
Isaac Williams   }

True Bill.   John Stewart, F. man

The State }
   vs   } Indictment Riot
Forrester Upshaw }
Parsons Upshaw }
& Adkins Upshaw }

True Bill.   John Stewart, F. man

The State }
   vs   } Charge Larceney
William Traylor & }
Thomas Hudspeth }

No Bill.   John Stewart, F. man

The State }
   vs   } Charge Larceney
John Stiles & }
Agness Stiles }

No Bill.   John Stewart, F. man

Geo Nailer }
   vs   } Case
Thomas Terry }

Jury Sworn

1. Richard Boland	5. Solomon Burford	9. Abel Gower
2. William Johnson	6. John Jackson	10. Pascal Traylor
3. James Cowin	7. Michael Wright	11. John Tarver
4. Abraham Zuber	8. James Kenney	12. Edward Powell

Is The Jury Who Returned the Following Verdict.

We, the Jury, find for the plaintiff Eighty Dollars, With Interest & Cost of Suit.

John Tarver, F. man

50

George Nailer }
      vs   } Case
John Garrett & }
Walton Whatley }

Dismis^d at the Defendant's Cost.

The State }   [58]
      vs   }
Elias Hines }

Jeffrey Early And Humphrey Edmonson Came into Court And Acknowledged Themselves Bound in the Sum of Two hundred dollars Each for the Appearance of the Defendant from Day to day during this Term.

Holeman Freman }
      vs   } Attachment
Robert Smith   }

Dismis^d.

Fredrick Boland }
      vs   }
[blank] Emberson}

Dismis^d.

The State }
      vs   } Indictment Forgery
John Smith }

Came and Appeared in Open Court John Smith, principle, and William Smith, his Security, And acknowledged Themselves Indebted to His Excellency the Governor, the Said John Smith in the Sum of One Thousand Dollars and the said William Smith in the Sum of five hundred Dollars, to be Void on Condition that, the Said John Smith Doth Appear to the Above Indictment, Stand Trial, and is discharg^d by the Due Course of Law on Saturday Next.

Test. Wm Hay, Clk   John Smith
                                            William Smith

The Court Then Adjourned untill Tomorrow Ten O'Clock. [59]

Ben Taliaferro

Friday September the 30th 1796

The Court Met According to Adjournment. Present, Judge Taliaferro.

Joseph Williams }
& Others }
vs } Caveat against the Will of Testament
the Executors of } of Browning Williams
Browning Williams }

It is Agreed by the Said Joseph Williams Others that the Said Caveat be withdrawn & the Said Will Carried into full Efect and Opperation, on Consideration whereof the Executors of Morgin Williams do hereby Agree that a Certain Bill of Sail Baring Date on the 22nd march 1785, from Joshua Bagley, of North Carolina, to the Said Morgan Williams, be Considered as if made to the afores^d Browning Williams, and that the Said Negroes mentioned in the Said Bill of Sail And their Increase be Distributed Agreably to the Will of the Said Browning Williams, And for the True and faithful performance of the Agrement, the Said Joseph Williams And Others on the One part and the Executors of Morgan Williams on the Other part Bind themselves, their Heirs, Executors, Administrators, Each to the Other, in the penalty of Two Thousand Dollars, & which further Considered that this Agrement be entered of Record

And Considered as the Judgment of the Court. [60]

In Testimony Whereof, the parties to these Presents do hereunto Interchangably Set there hands and Affix there Seals this 30th September 1796.

Acknowledged in }
Open Court 30th Sep^{tr} 1797 }
W. Hay, Clk }

Joseph Williams
George Sorrel &
Benjamin Bridges
John Williams
Tabitha Williams
Frances X Williams, her mark
Jno Fluker
John Boles
Sarah Williams

The State   }
    vs   } Indictment Forgery
John Callier }

Discarged on proclemation.

Henry Garrot   }
    vs   } Attachment
Thomas Johnson }

Jury Sworn

1. Abel Gower	5. Solomon Burford	9. Michael Wright
2. Saml Shannon	6. Nedham Norris	10. James Kenny
3. James Cowin	7. John Jackson	11. Thomas Moody
4. Abra Zuber	8. Zadock Barnet	12. John Gosdin

We, the Jury, find for the plaintiff four hundred and Twenty Eight Dollars & fifty Eight Cents.

James Kenney, F. man

John Doe, on the Demise }   [61]
of Edmonds Alaxander   }
      vs   } Ejectment
Richard Roe &   }
Jeffrey Early   }

We Find for the Plaintiff the Land in dispute, With Cost.

James Kenney, F. man

Richard Smith, on the   }
Demise of Henry D. Downs }
      vs   } Ejectment
Henry Read   }

The Death of the Real Defendant Hill Sugested.

Newal Walton }
    vs   } Case
John Andrews }

Jury Sworn

1. John Kenney	5. John Tarver	9. Samuel Moore
2. William Easter	6. Wm Duncan	10. Obediah Belcher
3. Ja^s Embry	7. John Shropshire	11. Richard Boland
4. John Hubbard	8. John Embry	12. Ge^o Williams

We, the Jury, find for the Plaintiff Thirty Nine Dollars & Eighteen Cents, With Costs.

John Shropshire, F. man

Richard Baily }
    vs   } Debt
James Kenney & }
Samuel Patton }

I, the Defendant, & we, Jessee Pye and and Robert Kenney, Acknowledge Our Selves Jointly and Severally bound to the Plaintiff in the Sum mentioned in the bail bond on condition, if the defendant Shall be cast in this Suit, we will pay the Condemnation money, or Surrender him as the law directs, or we will do it for him. Taken and Acknowledged in Open Court.

Wm Hay, Clk

James Kenney
Jessee Pye
Robert X Kenney, his mark

The State }   [62]
    vs   }
John Sellers }

We, Obediah Owns and Maliciah Reaves, Do bind Ourselves Jointly and Severally In the Sum of five hundred dollars Each, Condition To be Void on the

Said Obediah Owns Appearing Tomorrow morning at Nine O'clock to give Evidence In the Above Case in behalf of the Defendant.

Friday Sep^t 30th 1796   Obediah Owen
Wm Hay, Clk   Mallachi Reaves

John Hines }
    vs   } Case
Eps Tatum   }

Same Jury as in the Case of the State vs Callier.

We, the Jury, find for the Plaintiff Thirty four Dollars & Twenty five Cents, With Cost of Suit.

                              James Kenney, F. man

The State   }
    vs   } Indictment Larceney
William Jones }

The Prisonner being brought to the barr to be Tried. The Same Jury as in the Case Newel Walton vs John Andrews Returned the following Verdict.

Not Guilty.   John Tarver, F. man

                    Report of the Grand Jury

Absent John Stewart, F. man.

Present Joel Barnet, F. man.

The State   }   [63]
    vs   } Indictment Larcenny
Smith Alaxander   }

No Bill.   Joel Barnet, F. man

The State   }
    vs   } Indictment Assault
Plesent Compton }

no Bill.   Joel Barnet, F. man

The State   }
     vs   } Indictment Selling Liquors
James Kenney }

True Bill.   Joel Barnet, F. man

The State   }
     vs   } Indictment Maiham
Passons Upshaw }

True Bill.   Joel Barnet, F. man

The State   }
     vs   } Indictment Trespass
Joseph Alaxander}

No Bill.   Joel Barnet, F. man

The State   }
     vs   } Indictment Assault
Thomas Terry }

No Bill.   Joel Barnet, F. man

Joel Hurt   }
     vs   } Debt
James Murphey }

The same Jury as in the Case the State vs John Callier.

Returned the following Verdict. We, the Jury, do find for the plaintiff Eighty five
Dollars, with Interest on the Note & Cost of Suit.

                                             James Kenney, F. man

John Lindsey}   [64]
     vs   } Debt
Charles Burk }

Continued on Affidavit of Def^dt.

The State   }
    vs   } Indictment Purgery
Elias Hines }

The Prisoner being brought to the Barr to be Tried, the following Was Sworn.

(To Wit)

1. John Hollaway	5. John Tarver	9. Richard Bowland
2. William Easton	6. Wm Duncan	10. Wm Jinnings
3. Joseph Embry	7. Ja^s Embry	11. Wm Johnson
4. John Hubbard	8. Saml Moore	12. Isaac Penington

And Returned The Following Verdict. Not Guilty.

Court Adjourned until Nine O'clock Tomorrow Morning.

Ben Taliaferro

Saturday 1th of October 1797

The Court Met According to Adjournment. Present, Judge Taliaferro.

The State   }
    vs   } Indictment Horse Stealing
John Sellers }

The Prisoner being Brought To the Barr & the Following Jury Sworn.

1. Forrester Upshaw	5. Isaac Penington	9. Ge^o Williamson
2. Samuel Smith	6. Wm Smith	10. Saml Moore
3. John McWherter	7. Edward Powell	11. Chatt Scoggin
4. Taply Flint	8. Burwell Brewer	12. Andrew Bell

We, The Jury, find the Prisoner at The Barr Not guilty.

The State   } [65]
    vs   } Indictment Forgery
John Smith }

Indictment Quashed and the prisoner Discharged.

William Thompson }
     vs   } Appeal
Alaxander Gordon }

Special Jurors

1. Joel Barnett	5. Thomas Mereweather	9. James Parks
2. John Dun	6. John Milner	10. Wm Bledsoe
3. Thomas Gilmer	7. Ric^d Hartsfield	11. Saml Colquit
4. William Potts	8. William Strawther	12. Jno Peacock

We, the Jury, find no Cause of Suit.

Thos Gilmer, F. man

Thomas Simonton }
     vs   } Appeal
William Potts   }

Special Juriors

1. Thomas Gilmer	5. William Bledsoe	9. Charles Smith
2. Ric^d Hartsfield	6. William Strawther	10. John Peacock
3. Thos Meariweather	7. Saml Colquit	11. John Milner
4. James Parks	8. William Pace	12. Thos Loyd

The Jury Returned The following Verdict. We, the Jury, find no Cause of Suit.

Thos Gilmer, F. man

The State   }   [66]
     vs   } Indictment Selling Liquor
James Kinney }

James Kenney, the Defendand, & John Holliway Came into Open Court And Acknowledged themselves Indebted to his Excellency the Governor, the Said James Kenney in the Sum of One Thousand Dollars & John Holloway in the Sum of five hundred Dollars, To be Void on Condition that the Said James Kenney do Appear to the Above Indictment at the Next Superior Court to be held And Abide

58

the Judgment of Said Court, then the Above Obligation to be Void, Otherwise to Remain in full force & Virtue.

Test. W. Hay   James Kenney
                                                John Holloway

Ordered, that All Recognizances be Continued till The Next Term.

The Grand Jury made the Following presentments, Which was ordered to be published, Together with the Judge's Charge.

We, the Grand Jury, present the Surveyors of the Road leading from Phinizy's to Joseph Staton's.

We, the Grand Jury, present the Surveyors of the Road leading from the Cherokee Corner by this place.

We, the Grand Jury, present Abner James James for retailing liquors Without Licence & keeping a disorderly house.

We, the Grand Jury, Present as a greavance that we have not our   [67]
Courthouse and Goal built.

We, the Grand Jury, present as a Greavance that we have Not a publick bridge on the dry fork of long Creek, where the road leading from this place crossing the dry fork at James Rutledge's.

We, the Grand Jury, present that the patroll Law is not more Strictly Attended to.

We, the Grand Jury, present as a greavance that we have Not a Publick bridge on the dry fork of long Creek, Where the Roade crossing the Creek leading from Allen's Old Iron Works to Washington.

We, the Grand Jury, present a list of Defaulters Delivered to us by the Receiver of Tax Returns.

We, the Grand Jury, Return our Greatfull Thanks to Our last Legislature for there Zeal and Fidelity in favour of the inhabitants of this State, Supresing an Inequitious Act passed at Augusta the Seventeenth of January One thousand Seven hundred & Ninety five for disposing of Our Western Territory.

We, the Grand Jury, return Our most Gratfull to his Honor the Judge for his Juditious Charge given us & Receommend it to be published in the State Gazette, Together With these Our presentments.

Joel Barnett, F. man	William Strawther	Jn° Stewart	[68]
Thomas Dun	John Dunn	William Walker	
Jn° Milner	Charles Smith	Thomas Loyd	
James Parks	William Potts	Sam¹ Colquit	
Richard Hartsfield	William Bledsoe	Jn° Peacock	
John Fleming	Thomas Gilmer	John Smith	
William Pace			

Gentlemen of the Grand Jury,

I am afraid that the present Superior Court Term will Afford too many Proofs of the Ill Effects Resulting from the delays that have Taken place In fixing the Seat of Your Publick buildings, it Requires but Discernment to See the Impossibillitys of Conducting the business of Your County With that Order, propriety, and deceny that is Absolutely Necessary to Enable Your Courts to Render that Substantial, to Which (Agreeable to Our Laws) every Citizen has an Equal and Undoubted Right. What Must be the Impressions of Every Reflecting man, When he beholds the most Respectable and Devout Citizens of his County Approaching a Court of Justice through Tumult and Confusion to Contend for the most Sacred and Important of his Rights, And When he has Reached his point, he is Unable to Distinguish the Court from the Jury, or the Jury from the Croud, and After having Urged his Cause & fully Shewn the Justice of his demand, the Jury have to Retire to the Woods to make up their minds, without a roof to Cover them from the Weather, or What is of greater Importance

Exposed to the Importunities, either of the parties themselves or their   [69] friends, by Which means every Improper Impression may at Times be made on Jurors.

Gentlemen, a Few and Important Administrations of the Law Ought to be the Object of All the Different Departments of the Government, it is that by Which the Citizens is protected in his person, his property, and his Reputation. And by Which even Liberty it Self is Secured. it is True theer is a kind of licentious Liberty without Law, to Which in Civilised Countries even Slavery itself Ought to be Prefered, but the only Libertys worth the care of an Enlightened people is that by Which is Secured by Law, which no man dare Violate With impunity. As these are Objects (however desireable) that Cannot be Attained Without a Courthouse, where Your business may be Conducted With propriety, and a Substantial Goal for Confinement of Offenders, it is hoped that the Grand Jury will use their utmost influence to to remove the Several Dificulties that have Occured and that the Commissioners & Judges of Your County's Court, to Whoom the business has been Commited by the Legislature, Will proceed to fix perminently the place and errect Your publick buildings without further delay. When I reflect on the Oppulence and Respectability of your County, I am persuaded that the Only Dificulty is a difference of Opinion between the people living in the Two extreems of the County and I have understood that the Two places contended for Are Not more than Two miles Distance from each Other.

This is a difference Two Trifling to Occation a moments delay.   [70]
That Place which Afords the most Commodious Situation for building & the best warter Ought to be the place prefered. I consider this as a business that Demands your particular Attention & I have No Doubts but You Will Express your Sentements fully on the Subjects. And your Opinions cannot fail to have a good effect With the Commissioners. The Expence can hardly be an Object, as the commissioners have the right to draw from the funds of the State the Sum of One hundred pounds at any time they will apply, Which itself will be Sufficient for building a Very Convenient Courthouse.

I Will now, Gentlemen, call your Attention to Situation of your publick Roads and bridges. When you Reflect in your Remote Situation from market and that the people of Your County draws no benefit or advantage from Navagation. And, of Course, we Are Oblige to depend Intirely on the Roads for carrying there produce to market. and When we Consider further that the Season has Just arived for Carrying down the Present Crop of Tobacco & Cotton. I have no doubt but Will Examine with Care the Situation of the Severall Roads leading to market & will present the Several by Name, that they may be proceeded Against as the Law Directs.

To Enumerate the Severall Offences that Requires the Attention of the   [71]
Grand Jury woud be Trespassing on Your time Unnessarily, as it is well known that every Violation of Law, every breach of the peace, and every thing of Notorious Ill Example are punishable and Ought to be perticularly Noticed by the Grand Jury. Unlicened, disorderly Tipling houses I consider [blank] of Vice & immorrallity & I hope keepers of each, if any, will Not Escape Your Notice.

61

There is One Maxim which prevails in All Countries. Where Virtue and Respect for the Laws are Considered as Assential to the peace and hapiness of Society, which is that Every man Who Knowingly Violates the Laws, or Artfully elludes them, is in a State of Warr with Society And Renders himself unworthy the benevolence And Esteem of Mankind in as much as the Interest of every man is Injured thereby. of Course, Such Ought Not to escape the Punishment due to there Crimes. Suffer this maxim Gentlemen To Regulate Your Conduct and you will act Wisely.

Benjamin Taliaferro

Grand Jurors Drawn for Next Term [72]

William Harvie	Warren Stone	Hugh Ector
Charles Cargile	William Smith	John Lumpkin
Nicholas Hopson	Charles Darrity	Mical Whatley
William Berry	Winkfield Shropshire	Thomas Duke
John Garrett	William Strong	Benjamin Blake
Joshua Martin	Robert Haynes	John Prior
Micajah Mageehee	Paul Patrick	William Stewart
Charles Burk	Mathew Raines	Alaxander Read
John Devenport	Andrew Bell	Anthoney Ollive
Micajah Clark	Ge° Mathews	Isaac Collier
Joseph Martin	Burwell Pope	
Eps Tatum		

Pettit Jurors

Thomas Tugle	Jesse Willingham	John Gunnalds
John Leftridge	Jacob Larrance	Thomas Hendon
Charles Edmonson	Sam¹ Smith	James Sanders
Aron Johnston	William Gholsbey	Jeremiah Baugus
Zaccariah Larrance	K. Bohanan	Robert Taylor
William Smith	John Kelough	Taply Flint
William Morgin	Hawkins Bullock	Richard Reynolds
Dread Thornton	Hen Johnson	William Lasley
James Hines	Alax Morrowson	Britton Sanders
David Mcintosh	Ge° Cross	John Payne
John Richerson	William Ealey	Sherwood Wilkerson
Nathan Severson	John Britton	Joseph Baugh

Willis Perry	John Ponder	Lewis Grands
James Hukally	Jacob Everhart	Joseph Fenly
William Perkins	John Beasley	John Morgin
James Glenn	Mat Clendennal	Isaak Read
William Walker	Giles Thompkins	Mical Rign
Joel Hurt	Jessee Lee	Ge° Doggit
John Stiles	Thomas [blank]	Johnson Clark
	William Vere	James Magnon
	John Kane	

The Court Then Adjourned untill Court in Course.   [73]

Ben Taliafferro

March Term 1797

At a Superior Court Begun & held ~~in & for the~~ In and for the County of Oglethorpe on the 28th of March 1797. Present, His Honour Judge Taliaferro.

Grand Jury Sworn

1. Nicholas Hopson, FM	8. John Garrett	15. Micajah Clark
2. William Strong	9. Joshua Martin	16. Thomas Johnson
3. Mathew Raines	10. Charles Burk	17. Anthoney Ollive
4. William Berry	11. Robert Haynes	18. William Stewart
5. Isaac Collier	12. Charles Cargile	19. Joseph Horton
6. Warren Stone	13. Eps Tatum	20. Hugh Ector
7. Andrew Bell	14. William Smith	

Obediah Belcher   }
        vs   } Case
Robert Beckers &   }
William McGibberney }

Charles Burk & Peter Cartright Came into Court and Acknowledged Themselves Special Bail in the Above Case Agreeable to the Rules of Court.

Epps Tatum   }
        vs   } Debt
Benjamin Stringfellow }
& William Casey   }

Dismised.

John Buckner   }   [74]
        vs   } Case
James Devenport }

James Devenport, Jun[r] and James Devenport, Sen[r] Came into Court and
Acknowledged Themselves Special Bail in the Above Case Agreeable to the
Rules of Court.

James Devenport, Jun[r]
James Devenport, Sen[r]

Administrators of}
Edward Brewer   }
        vs   } Case
Grant Taylor   }

Dismised.

John Blanton   }
        vs   } Ejectment
William Merritt }

Jury Sworn

1. Aaron Johnson	5. Henry Johnson	9. John Ponder
2. Zach Lawrance	6. Robert Taylor	10. Jacob Averhart
3. Jessee Willingham	7. Mark Riggin	11. Jeremiah Boggus
4. Jacob Lawrance	8. William Gholsbey	12. Tapley Flint

We, the Jury, Find for the Plaintiff the Land Contended for and Cost of Suit.

Jessee Willingham, F. man

The State   }
        vs   } Indictment Horse Stealing
John Hopper }

We, the Jury, find the Within a True Bill.

Nicholas Hopson, F. man

John Michael, Surviving}   [75]
Partner of Michael   }
        vs   } Case
Charles Sims   }

I do hereby Confess Judgment for the Sum of One hundred & Twenty One Dollars, on Stay of Execution untill the Twenty fifth day of December Next, With Interest Untill paid.

Test. Jn° Sims   Charles X Sims, his mark

Court then Adjourned untill Ten O'Clock Tomorrow.

Ben Taliaferro

Richard Smith   }
ex dem Jeffrey Early }
      vs   }
William Stiles &   }
Andrew Pickens   }

on Motion of Mr Carnes, it is Ordered that Andrew Pickings be made Defendant in this Case, by Consent of parties And Assent of the Court, it is Ordered that a resurvey of the Land in dispute Shall be made by the Surveyor of Oglethorpe County. Each party, or his Attorney, having Twenty days Notice of the time of Such Survey & that the Said Surveyor Asertain a fair plat, the Interferences & protentions of Each party, & how each Survey is particularly bounded, & Return the Plat So made Out under his hand & Seal to the Clerk of this Court on or before the first day of the Next Term.

James Parks }   [76]
     vs   } Case
Elisha Hunter }

28th day of March 1797

I do, herby Virtue of a power of Attorney To me As Well as Others Directed And herewith filed, Appear for the Defendant and Confess Judgment for the Sum of five hundred Dollars, ~~With Interest~~ With Interest from the Twenty fifth day of December last.

Micajah Williamson, Def^{ts} Att^y

Wednesday 29th the Court Met According to Adjournment. Present, Judge Taliaferro.

John Hines }
   vs   }
Royal Clay }

Jury Sworn

1. Jacob Lorance	5. Britain Sanders	9. William Goolsbey
2. Henry Johnson	6. Mark Riggin	10. John Ponder
3. Aaron Johnson	7. Dread Thornton	11. Jeremiah Boggus
4. Jessee Willingham	8. John Stiles	12. Tapley Flint

Are the Jury Who Returned the following.

We, the Jury, find for the Plaintiff Twenty Dollars & Cost.

Jessee Willingham, Forman

Thomas Dunn   } These three persons, being of the Original pannel of the
Michael Whatley } Grand Jury, Came into Court & wer quallified as Such.
Phillip Edmonson}

The State   }   [77]
     vs   } Indictment Assault
Godfrey Adams }

We, of the Jury, do find the within a True Bill.

N. Hopson, F. man

The State   }
     vs   } Ind^t Assault
John Shropshire }

We, of the Jury, do find the Within Not to be a True Bill.

                              N. Hopson, F. man

The State   }
     vs   } Ind^t Assault
John Fleming }

We, of the Jury, do find the Within Not to be a True Bill.

                              N. Hopson, F. man

The State   }
     vs   } Ind^t Assault
John Fleming }

We, of the Jury, do find the Within a True Bill.

                              N. Hopson, F. man

The State   }
     vs   } Ind^t Larcenny
Jessee Wilks & }
John Wilks   }

We, of the Jury, do find the Within Not to be a True Bill.

                              N. Hopson, F. man

Thomas Dunn Excused from the Jury.

James McCoy   }   [78]
     vs   } Case
Jeffrey Early }

1. William McCrie	5. Ge° Cross	9. James Northington
2. James Stovall	6. Cordy Pate	10. Zacheas Wilson
3. Jo^s Wilson	7. James Hines	11. Humphrey Edmonson
4. James Glenn	8. William Johnson	12. David McCord

Are the Jury Who Returned the Following.

We, the Jury, find for the Plaintiff Forty Two Dollars 6¼ Cents, being the Amount of Principle & Interest due, With Cost of Suit.

W^m McCrie, F. man

James McCammon }
     vs   } Case
Winkfield Shropshire }
& John Shropshire }

I hereby Confess Judgment to The Administrators of James McCammon for One hundred and fifty four Dollars & Six & a quarter Cents, With Stay of Execution untill the 25th day of December Next, With Interest & Cost of Suit, Which may be Discharged With Three Thousand Six hundred & thirty Three pounds of Augusta Inspected Crop Tobacco, if paid on or before that time. March 29th 1797

Attest. John Hardeman   John Shropshire

James Gillaspell   }   [79]
     vs   } Debt
Hannah McCartney, Adm^x }
of Daniel McCartney, Dec^d }

Dismis^d.

John Towns   }
     vs   } Debt
Harrison Musgrove & }
Jinsey Williams, Exec^{ts} }

We, the Parties Litigant in the Above case, agree to Leave All matters in dispute to the Award and Arbitrament of Mathew Talbot, David Terrill, Edmond Daniel,

John Stewart, & Daniel price, or Any three of them, Whose Award Shall be made the Judgment of the Court, provided the Said Award be Returned to the Next Superior Court for Oglethorpe County. the Arbitrators Are to meet at Spencer Branham's in Wilkes County on the third day of July Next, in Order to Settle the dispute As Afores^d, With power to Adjourn from day to day untill they do make theire Award On the Next term of the Superior Court for the County of Oglethorpe.

Micajah Williamson, Pllf^s Att^y
Jno Mathews, Def^{ts} Att^y

The Court then Adjourned untill Ten O'Clock Tomorrow.

Ben Taliaferro

Thursday The 30th The Honorable Court Met According to Adjournment.   [80] Present, His Honor Ben Taliaferro.

James Marbry }
    vs   }
Jeffrey Early }

Jeffrey Early, being Dissatisfied With the Judgment in this case, Appeals, with John Floyd Security And binds themselves to pay the Eventual Condemnation money or to Surrender the principal in Execution.

Jeffrey Early
John Floyd

The Above Appeal Withdrawn April 5th 1797.

Rec^d Twenty Dollars & 25 Cents, Which he paid on the Above Appeal.

Christopher Orr }
    vs   }
Joseph Wilson }

Jurors

1. Zaccariah Lawrence	5. Henry Johnson	9. William Goolsbey
2. Jessee Willingham	6. Britton Sanders	10. John Ponder

| 3. Jacob Lawrence | 7. Mark Raggin | 11. Jeremiah Boggus |
| 4. James Glenn | 8. John Gunnalds | 12. Tapley Flint |

Are the Jury Who Returned the following Verdict.

We, the Jury, find for the plaintiff Seventy Two Dollars Principle, With Interest and Cost of Suit.

Jessee Willingham, F. man

William Johnson }   [81]
    vs   }
John W. Burnes }

I do hereby Appear and Confess Judgment for the Sum of One hiundred And fifteen dollars and Seventy five Cents in the Above Case, With Stay of Execution untill the Twenty fifth day of December Next, Which Said Sum Above mentioned may be Discharged With Tobacco at the Market price, With Interest And Cost.

M. Williamson, Defend^{ts} att^y

Upon Motion of John Griffin, Esqr, Attorney, Stating to the Court that Howell Tatum is the Executor of the Estate of Peter Tatum, Dec^d, And that there is probabillity that the Said Estate will be Wasted And Injured by the Said Howell Tatum, he Not having giving Sufficient Security, the Said Howell Tatum, by his Consent, came into Court and gave Two good Securities Each in One Thousand Dollars & the Said Howell Tatum in Two thousand Dollars Agreable to the foregoing, the Said Howell Tatum Acknowledged himself indebted to the heirs & Representatives & Distributees of the Said Peter Tatum, Dec^d in the Sum of Two Thousand Dollars And John Garrott, his Security in One Thousand Dollars, & William Ragsdale, his Other Security, in the Sum of One thousand Dollars, Also to be Recovered of the Said Several persons by the Said Representatives, provided the Said Howell Tatum fails to perform his duty as Executor of the Estate of Peter Tatum, Dec^d Aforesaid from this time foreward. Witness their hands this 30th day of March 1797

Acknowledged in Open Court   Howell Tatum
John Hardeman, for Wm Hay, Clk   John Garrott
                                 William Ragsdale

Ahemalick Hawkins }
    vs   } Trover
Daniel Roberts   }

Jurors

1. George Cross	5. Chatten Scroggin	9. Richard Thornton
2. James Macby	6. Woody Taylor	10. Harroson Lumpkin
3. John Legit	7. Robt Gillaspie	11. Henry Haynes
4. Robert Lumpkin	8. Jessee Pye	12. Zac Wilson

Are the Jury Who Returned the following.

We, the Jury, find for the Plaintiff Sixty Dollars, with Costs.

Chatten Scroggin, F. man

The State   }
    vs   } Indictment Counterfeiting a guinea
Leroy Upshaw }

We, of the Jury, do find the Within a True Bill.

Nicholas Hopson, F. man

The State   }
    vs   } Indictment Larceney
William Rogers }

We, of the Jury, find the Within Not to be a True Bill.

Nicholas Hopson, F. man

Charles Finch }
    vs   } Ejectment
Ratsford Holt }

Continued on Affidavit of the Plaintiff.

The State   }
    vs   } Ind^t
Leroy Upshaw }

We, John Grisham & Jessee Willingham, Do bind Our selves Jointly & Severally In the Sum of five hundred dollars Each.

Condition to be Void on the Said John Gresham Appearing on Saturday at Ten O'Clock to give Evidence in the Above Case in behalf of the State.

Jn° Gresham
Jessee Willingham

Elisha Brewer & }
Lemuel Black }
   vs }
Avington McElroy }

Jurors

1. Zac Larance	5. Henry Johnson	9. Dread Thornton
2. Jessee Willingham	6. Britton Sanders	10. Jn° Ponder
3. Jacob Lorance	7. Mark Ragan	11. Jar^h Boggus
4. James Glenn	8. William Goolsbey	12. Tapley Flint

Are The Jury Who Returned the Following.

We, the Jury, find find for the plaintiff Two hundred And Twenty Six Dollars Ninety Three Cents, With Interest & Cost of Suit.

Jessee Willingham, Fm

Sarah Alaxander, as }
next freind to Joseph & }
Smith Alaxanders, Minors }
   vs } Fals Imprisonment
William Johnson & }
Noel Thornton }

(See fors[blot]

Jurors   [84]

1. James Macbee	5. John Legett	9. Saml Moore
2. Woody Taylor	6. Harrason Lumpkin	10. Zac Wilson

3. Robert Lumpkin	7. John Floyd	11. Edward Moore
4. Henry Haynes	8. Ge^o Cross	12. William Bledsoe

Are the Jury Who Returned the following Verdict.

We, the Jury, find for the Plaintiff One hundred Dollars, with Cost of Suit.

Edward Moore, F. man

John Blanton }
    vs   } Ejectment
William Merritt }

William Merritt, being Dissatisfied With the Verdict in this case, and prays an Appeal and Comes With Michael Whatley, Esqr, as his Security, & the Said William Merritt & the Said Michael Whatley, Esqr bind themselves to pay the eventual condemnation money, if The Said Merritt Should be Cast in his Suit, or to Surrender the Defendant in Discharge thereof. And the Cost Paid.

William Merritt
Michael Whatley

Charles Finch }
    vs   } Ejectment
Ratsford & Holt }

Upon Motion of John Griffin, Att^y for Plaintiff, it is Ordered that a rule of Survey be Granted to the Plaintiff & that the Surveyor of the County be Required to Attend the Plaintiff to lay Out

And Admeasure the land in dispute, the Plaintiff first Giving Notice   [85] to the Defendant, and Return a plat of the Same, With Remarks Shewing Wheather it Appears Within the Boundary Caled for, & how it Interferes With the land of Defendant, and how much the plaintiff & Defendant Are Intitled, Each to have an Attending Surveyor if they may think proper, Whose Return With that of the Surveyor Certifyed by Each of them Will be Received as Evidence on the Trial, and the Said Return must be made before the Next Term.

James Stallings }
    vs   } Case
Archer Norris }

The Same Jury as in the Case of Elisha Brown & Lemuel Black vs Avington McElroy. Who Returned the following. We, the Jury, find for the Plaintiff One hundred & One Dollars & Seventy Eight Cents ¾, With Interest And Cost.

Jessee Willingham, F. man

Christopher Orr }
     vs }
Joseph Wilson }

Joseph Wilson, Together With James Brook, Came into Court bound themselves in the Sum of One hundred Dollars, it being for the Stay of Execution Sixty days in the above Case.

Joseph Wilson
James X Brooks, his mark

Sarah Alaxander }   [86]
     vs }
Noel Thornton and }
William Johnson }

We, Noel Thornton & William Johnson, And John Smith, Security, Came Into Court and bound themselves in the Sum of One hundred & fifty Dollars, it being for the Stay of Execution Sixty days in the Above Case.

Replevy Withdrawn }   Noel Thornton
And Appeal Entered }   William Johnson

The Court Then Adjourned untill Ten O'Clock Tomorrow Morning.

Ben Taliaferro

Friday the 31st the Honorable Court met According to Adjournment. Present, his Honor Ben Taliaferro.

West Harris }
     vs } Sheriff's Report
James Shorter & }
Jeffrey Early }

Setled.

John Letwich }
    agt[s]   } Appeal
Richard Maleir }

The Death of the Appellant Suggested.

Commissioners of the }
Town of Washington }
       vs   } Sheriff's Report
James Hart and   }
John Marrain   }

Levey Withdrawn.

Travis C. Traylor }   [87]
    vs   } Case
William Strother }

Setled.

Sam[l] Read   }
    vs   } Case
Christopher Irvin   }
& Nathaniel Porter }

Setled.

Thomas McAlpin }
& Others   }
    vs   } Ejectment
William Edwards }

By Assent of the Court, Addam Simmons, Next friend to the heirs & Representatives of Robert Pougue, Dec[d], Comes Into Court & is made Defendant as Next friend Aforesaid in the Place and Stead of William Edwards, Tenant in Possession, and the usual Rule Entered into.

Bailey   }
  vs   }
Kenney & Patton }

The Plaintiff Came Into Court & And Acknowledged himself fully Satisfied, The Principal, Interest, and Cost being Paid.

Henry Johnson }
    vs   } Case
Thomas Johnson }

By Virtue of a Power of Attorney to be Directed And herewith filed, I do hereby Appear for the Defendand and Confess Judgment to the plaintiff for the Sum of five Thousand four hundred Dollars and Cost of Suit.

Test. R. Walker   J. L. Walton, for Def[t]

Charles Burk }   [88]
    vs   } Ejectment
Stephen Herd }

On Motion of M[r] Griffin, Attorney for for the Plaintiff, it is Ordered that a Survey be made as well of the lands in dispute as of the Time of the Old Ceded Lands, from the head of Ogeechee to the Buffalow lick, as Run by the White people and Indians in the Year 1773.

In Conformity to the Treaty made that Year, that the County Surveyor be Appointed on the Part of the Court & borth Parties Are at liberty to have an Assistant Surveyor and that they be governed by the best Information they Can Obtain from the Pilots Who ware present at running the said line or from Such of them as Can be got to Attend, Who Shall be Sworn to give Just and True Information to the Said Surveyor, and it is further Ordered, that Ten days Previous Notice Shall be given to the Oposite parties at the Time of proceeding to the Making of Said Survey, Respectively.

Thomas McAlpin   }
    vs   } Ejectment
Adam Simmons   }
next friend to the   }
Heirs of Pougue, Dec[d]}

Upon motion of Mr Griffin, Attorney for plaintiff, a Rule of Survey is Granted and the County Surveyor Required to Attend the Plaintiff and lay out and admeasure the Said land Cleared by plaintiff and Return the Same at the Next Term, Ten days Notice Must be given Either partie, Who may Take Each an Attending Surveyor, the Return to be Made at the Next Term.

The State }   [89]
  vs   } Ind^t Horse Stealing
John Hopper }

The Prisoner being Brought to the Barr, Plead not guilty.   Posponed till Tomorrow.

Grand Jurors Drawn For the Next Term

John Banks	Joseph Parks	Samuel Strong
Isam Hendon	Jonathan Baird	Richard Gooldsbey
Osnan Whatley	James Horton	Permenus Haynes
Isaak Goolsbey	Thomas Black	Robert Beavers
Clifton Wood Roof	John Marks	John Moore
Ezekel Gillum	Guy Smith	William McElrory
Thomas Scoggin	James Rutledge	John Fluker
William Hendon	Miles Ginnings	Richard Harvie
Robert Cruchfield	Humphrey Edmonson	George Cowin
Thomas Johnson	George Swain	Jeffrey Easly
Isaak Hail	Thomas Simonton	Benjamin Balcher
	John Griffin	

Petit Jurors

Holeday Newson	Robert Elliot	John Bridges
John Bailey	William Renfrow	Jacob Elsbury
Thomas Morgin	Isaac McElroy	John Thurmond
Daniel Goolsbey	Phillimon Bird	John Croley
William Duke	Jeremiah Wooton	Noah Hill
Noah Freman	Jessee Peters	John Sorrow
John Blakley	Reubin Embry	Isaac Kelough
Charles McCartney	Joseph James	Isaac Williams
Ben^j Edwards	Ethelord Crews	John Thomas
Howell Tatum	Edward Prior	Reubin Radford
John Williams	Levey Gally	John Acre

William Ramsey	William Yancey	Charles Sims
Middleton Brooks	William Freman	John Cole
Jacobus Watts	U. Smith	Nathaniel Bradford
Charles Hardman	Henry Johnson	Moses Ray
	Godfrey Hartsfield	James Thomson
	James McCarter	Jessee Pye
	John Ramsey	James Devenport

Henry Sorrow
Presley Thornton
John Peck
Thomas Norton
Ben^j Staton

The Court Then Adjourned Untill 9 O'Clock Tomorrow.   [90]

Ben Taliaferro

Saturday 1st day of April The Honorable Court Met According to Adjournment. Present, Judge Taliaferro.

Sarah Alaxander }
    vs   } Fals Imprisonment
William Johnson }
& Noel Thornton }

William Johnson & Noel Thornton, being Dissatisfied With the Judgment in this Case, Appeals With John Banks Security, and Bind themselves to Pay the Eventual Condemnation money or to Surrender the principal in Execution. Fees paid.

William Johnson
Noel Thornton
John Banks

The State   }
    vs   } Ind^t passing counterfeit guineas
Leroy Upshaw }

The Prisoner, being Brought to the barr for trial. The following Jury was Elected & Sworn.

1. Jacob Lorance	5. Mark Riggan	9. James Glenn
2. Jessee Willingham	6. John Stiles	10. Saml Whitehead
3. Henry Johnson	7. Jacob Everalt	11. Jessee Clay
4. George Cross	8. Jeremiah Boggus	12. Thomas Rutledge

We, the Jury, find Not guilty.

Jessee Willingham, Fman

The State   }
   vs   }
James Moore}

Recognizance Discharged.

The State   }   [91]
   vs   } Ind^t
Forrester Upshaw}

The Said Forrester Upshaw, being Three Times Solemnly Called and failing to Appear, And Beaverly Greenwood failing to produce the Body of the said Forrester Upshaw, Ordered that the Recognizance of the Said Forrester, Beaverly, & John, his Securities, be Estrated and that a Sire Facius Issue Against them, Returnable to the Next Term to Shew Cause, if Any they have, Why Judgment Should Not be entered Against them for the Amount thereof.

The State   }
   vs   } Ind^t
Forrester Upshaw }
& Pasons Upshaw }

The Said Forrester Upshaw & Passons Upshaw, being three times Solemnly Called and failing to Appear, And Beaverly Greenwood and Leroy Upshaw failing to produce the Bodies of the said Forrester & Passons Upshaw, Ordered that the Recognizance of the Said Forrester Upshaw, Passons Upshaw, & Beaverly Greenwood, & Leroy Upshaw Upshaw, their Securities, be Estraited and that a Sire Facius Issue Against them, Returnable to the Next Term to Shew Cause, if Any they have, Why Judgment Should Not be entered Against them for the Amount thereof.

The State }
  vs } Ind^t Horse Stealing
John Hopper }

The Prisoner being brought to the Barr for Trial, the following Jury were Elected & Sworn (To Wit).

1. Jessee Willingham 5. James Glenn 9. John Ponder
2. George Cross 6. John Sorrow 10. Jessee Wilks
3. Jacob Everart 7. Joseph Canterbury 11. Noel Thornton
4. Jeremiah Boggus 8. Plesent Cumtton 12. William Johnson

We, the Jury, find Not Guilty.

Stallings & Co }   [92]
  vs   }
Archer Norris }

I, Archer Norris, principal, & William Norris & Hardy Norris, Securities, Came Into Court and bound themselves in the Sum of One hundred & fifty Dollars Each, it being for the Stay of Execution Sixty days in the Above Case.

        Archer Norris
        William Norris
        Hardy Norris

The Court then Adjourned Untill Court in Course.

        Ben Taliaferro

James Magbee }
  vs } Case
Jeffrey Early }

James Magbee, being Dissatisfied With the Judgment in this case, Appear^d With Theophilus Allison, Security, Binds themselves to pay the Eventual Condemnation money or to Surrender the principal in Execution

        James Magbee
        Theop^s Allison

Hines }
  vs }
Clay }

I, Royal Clay, Principal, & Jessee Clay, Security, do bind ourselves Jointly and Severally in the Sum of One hundred Dollars Each, it being for the Stay of Execution Sixty days in the Above Case.

Royal Clay
Jessee Clay

Rec^d of Royal Clay fifty one dollars, being the Cost & Damage on the Above Suit.

W. Hay, Clk

Abemelick Hawkins }   [93]
     vs   } Case
Daniel Roberts   }

I, Joshua Askew, principal Agent for Daniel Robert, Being Dissatisfied With the Judgment in this Case, Appeard with Vallentine Geiger, Security, Bind themselves to pay the Eventual Condemnation money or to surrender the principal in Execution.

Joshua Askew
Vallentine Geiger

Rules for regulating the proceedings & Practices of the Superior Courts to be held in the Counties of this State.

The Stile of Address Shall be that Whach has been heretofore Customary.

The Principals of Admistion of Attorneys being Acknowledged of the Laws and the Practice of Courts, a Liberal Examination Shall be had in these Respects.

For the Sake of Decent Conformity to Ancient Custom In the Profession, the Attorneys Ought to be heard in a Black Robe, Especially in Criminal Cases, but this is Not to be Insisted on With those Who have not provided themselves With Such Ha[blot] untill the Second Term.

The Order of Pleading Shall Corraspond With that Laid Down by Judge Blackston, And in no Case Shall more than One of the Council be heard in Conclusion.

In Cases Where Bail is Required, the Sheriff Shall Take Bond in the usual form, With a Condition to the following.

Effect, that if the above bounden (the Defendant) do Appear at the Next   [94] Superior Court to be held in and for the County of [blank] on the [blank] day of [blank] Next to Answer the Plaintiff in an Action of [blank] Dollars (the Sum for Which Bail is Ordered), then this Obligation to be Void & of Non Effect, Otherwise to Remain in full force and Virtue, Sealed &c.

In Case of Special Bail, the Same Shall be Offered as the Law direct and Shall be Entered in the Court Book in the following Words, or to the like Effect. I, the Defendant, and we (the Securities), With their Additions, Acknowledge Ourselves Jointly and Severly bound to (the Plaintiff in the Sum of Mentioned in the Sheriff's Bond) on this Condition, that if the Defendant Shall be Cast in this Suit (he, the Defendant) Will pay the Condemnation money, or Surrender himself as the Law Directs, or we will do it for him. Taken & Acknowledged before &c A, B. & C.

And Exceptions to Special Bail Shall be Taken When the Same is Offered on Notice to the Plaintiff, or his Attorney. And the Same Shall be Perfected on or before the Rising of the Court, in default Whereof the Plaintiff Shall be at liberty to proceed on the Bail Bond by Assignment, Which Shall be made under the hand and Seal of the Sheriff in the presence of Two Witnesses in Words to the following Effect. I, [blank], Sheriff of the County of [blank], do hereby Assign, Transfer, And Set Over the Within Bond to the Plaintiff in the Within Mentioned Action. In Witness &c.

No Attorney or Other Officer of the Court Shall be Bail in any Suit   [95] or Action depending or determined in Court, and no Attorney Shall be permited to appear Either for plaintiff or Defendant Untill he produses a Warrent for that purpose.

Dockets of Original Writs and processes Shall be made out by the Clerk, Who Shall furnish a fair & Correct Copey for the Use of the Court and deliver the Same at the first Opening thereof. the Clerk Shall Also keep a remembrance book, Shall be Alphabetically Entered All Judgments Obtained in Court, And Shall Keep a Docket of All Executions, Which Shall be Caled the Execution Docket.

When the Plaintiff, or his Attorney, Shall Receive Satisfaction for debt or damage & Judgment & the Court, Satisfaction Shall be fourthwith Entered up by the plaintiff, or his Attorneys, on pain of being proceeded Against for a Contempt.

The Sheriff Shall make returns at the Opening of the Court of the names of the Justices, Correner, & Constables for their Respective Counties to the Clerk of the Court, Who Shall not depart therefrom Without leave.

The Justices of the peace Shall Deposit or Transmit to The Clerk of the Court, Attorney or Solicitor General all Information, Examinations, & Recognizance by them Taken at least one day before the Siting of the Court, and they direct all persons Who Shall be bound to Prosecute, that they Attend The Attorney or Solicitor or Attorney Genl on the first day of the Court.

In Any Case of Trial by Appeal before a Special Jury, it Shall not be in   [96] the power of the plaintiff to Claim the Right of Suffering a nonsuit, but the Verdict thereon Shall be final And Conclusive, to Which End there Shall be no necessity to Call the plaintiff When the Special Jury have returned there Verdict, the Appellant's Attorney being answerable for the fees.

The Juditiary Law having Taken away the Right of the Inferior Courts having Cognizance in the Trial of Real Estates, and as there are Suits of this Nature depending in Said Inferior Courts, and it Not being directed by Said Act in What manner Said Suits Shall be removed to the Superior Court, It is Ordered, that the following Mode be Observ^d, that is to say, the party desiring to remove the Cause Shall Take Out a Writ of Certiorari from the Clerk of the Superior Court, Which Writs Shall be made out of Courts Without Any delay. And the Same being Carried to the Clerk of the Inferior Court. All the proceedings Shall be Sent up to the Clerk's Office of the Superior Court, With a Return on the Certiorari. And there Upon, the Cause Shall be entered on the Docket of the Superior Court And Other proceedings Take place, as if the Suit had Originated there, but no Suit So Removed Shall be Allowed to Come to Trial Without a Written Notice of the Removal being given to the Opisite party, or his Attorney, if in the County, At least Twenty days before the meeting of the Court and Service of Such

Notice provided by Affidavit or Admited or in Case the Said Opposite   [97] party, or his Attorney, Shall Not Reside in the County Where the Said Cause Shall be depending, then the Said Notice Shall be published in One of the Publick Gazettes of this State At least Twenty days before the meeting of the Court and the Said publickation proved as aforesaid or Admitted in Cases of proceeding for foreclosing Mortgages of personal property, the party In possession Shall be liable to be held to bail to the Amount of the Debt Upon the Oath of the party Claiming, or his Attorney. When Cases in the first Instant required the Powers of a Court of Equity, the mode of proceedings Shall be by Bill or petition and the Usial process of Subpoena Shall Issue & Copies of Bill & Subpoenas Serv^d on the defendant, if in the State as in Common Cases, if Out of the State, the Subpoena Shall be published Six months in One of the publick Gazettes, to bring in the defendant to answer the defen^d, on Appearance Shall have Such Reasonable Time to Answer as the Court Shall find to be Equitable. When the Defendant Remains in Default or Contempt, the Plaintiff Shall be Intitled to have his petition or Bill to be Taken so far Confesed as to Justify An Interlocutory Order being passed thereon & Which Shall Intitle the Complainant to have his case Exparte Submited to the Jury, Who may Decree on the Merits of the Case laid before them.

All Causes at Common Law are directed are directed to Originate by   [98] Petition & process and Some of these cases may require Equitable Interposition. When a Common Law Remedy is Not Adequate, Either party, Plaintiff or Defendant, may State the facts Supported by Affidavit, of Which the Court Will Judge, and if the Application is Sustain^d, Either party Shall be compeled to Answer on Oath at Such Reasonable Time on Notice as may be deemed proper, so as no Unnessary Delay be Occationed. Subsequent proceedings Shall be the Same as in other Equity Cases. In regard to the Establishment of Copies of papers under the Act of the 22nd of February 1785, All Applications for the purpose Shall be made in Oppen Court Only, And Accompanied With Proof on Oath to the Satisfaction of the Court. the following is perscribed as the form of the rules Nisi, the Affidavit, and the Rule Absilute in Such Cases, that is to Say, the Rule Nisi. On the Petition of A. B., Statting that being possesed of a Note of hand, Signed C. D., Bearing date [blank] for the Sum of [blank] Dollars, a Copy Whereof, as Nearly as Your Petitioner Could recollect, Was Anaxed to the Said petition is Now lodged in the Clerk's Office, Together With an Affidavit, pursuant to the Act of the 22nd of February 1785, that the Said Note was lost or destroyed during the late Warr, and praying the benefit Intended by Said Act, and Other Circumstantial proof being Also laid before the Court.

It is Ordered, that the Said Note be Established as Directed by the Said   [99] Act, on the said A. B. his Publishing a Notice as therein required & for the Space of Six months in One of the Publick Gazetts of this State, Unless Cause Shall be Shewn to the Contrary Within the Six months, Or Other Matter Shall Appear to the Court Against the Same.

The Form of the Affidavit

State of Georgia }
[blank] County   } A. B., & C., Being Duly Sworn, Maketh Oath that Persuant
to a Rule of Court of the [blank] last In the Deponant did Cause to be published
for the Space of Six Months in the publick Gazetts of the Notice of his Intention
of Establishing a Note of hand, Signed C. D., bearing date [blank], for the Sum of
[blank] Dollars, a copy Whereof is filed in the Clerk's Office of the County,
Which Publication Will Appear by the Gazetts hereto Anaxed, And that no person
hath to the Deponant's Knowledge appeared to gainsay the Same.

Sworn to this [blank] Day of [blank] Before [blank].

The Rule Absolute

On Motion of Mr W., Council for A. B., refering to the rule of the last,
Accompanyed by an Affidavit of the Said A. B., that the Several matters Required
of him had been duly perfected, Which Affidavit remains Recorded in this Court.
It is Ordered, that the Said Rule Nisi become made Absolute, no person having
Appeared to gainsay the Same, & in Case Any person Shall Appear within the
time perscribed to gainsay the Establishment

of Such Papers, he Shall file his Objections in Writing in the Nature   [100]
of a Plea in the Clerk's Office. And the Said Petition and Plea Shall make a
record, on Which may be found an Issue of Either Law or fact According to
Circumstances.

The Mode of foreclosing Mortgages Shall be as heretofore, in Such Cases when
the State is a party. And the Rule Absolute in other Cases Varied so far as to
Direct Execution to Issue in Terms of the Judiciary Act.

Such Rules of Practice have been heretofore Adopted Not repugnant to the
Judiciary Law. And the foregoing Rules are Declared to be in force.

Done at Louisville the Nineteenth Day of July in the year of Our Lord One Thousand Seven hundred And Ninety Six.

William Stephens
Benjamin Taliaferro
Wm Few
D. B. Mitchell
H^y Cauldwell

At a Superior Court Begun and held for the County of Oglethorpe on the   [101] Twenty Eighth day of September 1797. Present, his Honor Judge Stephens.

The Commestion of his Honor the Judge and the Clause of the Judiciary Act, Which Direct the Judges to Attend, Being Read, Ordered that the Vinire of the Grand and Pettit Jury be Caled Over When the Judge Appeared. (Viz.)

John Lumpkin, Esquire Elected Clerk of the Superior Court, Appeared and Entered on the Duties of his Office.

Pettit Jury

1. Thomas Morgin	6. Edward Prior	11. John Sorrow
2. Noah Freman	7. Isaac Hodge	12. John Acre
3. Howell Tatum	8. Jacob Elsbury	13. Benjamin Staton
4. Middleton Brooks	9. Henry Johnson	14. Henry Sorrow
5. Reubin Embry	10. Noah Hill	15. Nathaniel Bradford

William Coats}
    vs   }
John Wooton }

Jury Sworn N° 1

1. Noah Freman	5. Edward Prior	9. John Sorrow
2. Howell Tatum	6. Isaac Hodge	10. John Acre
3. Middleton Brooks	7. Jacob Elsbury	11. Benajmin Staton
4. Reubin Embry	8. Noah Hill	12. Henry Sorrow

We find for the Plaintiff Eighty five Dollars Seventy Eight Cents, With Cost.

Isaac Hodge, F. man

Grand Jurors Sworn

John Ramsey	Jn° Moore	Thomas Moodey
Robert Beavers	Permenus Haynes	Robert Haynes
John Banks	Ezekel Gillum	Abram Eason
Clifton Woodroff	James Rutledge	John Fluker
Thomas Morgin	William Hendon	Thomas Doggit
Thomas Johnson	Andrew Bell	Saml Strong, Excused
John Marks	David Weaver	from the Grand Jury for
Samuel Strong	Osnan Whatley	the present Term
Richard Goolsby	James Thomas	James Thomas Chosen
		F. man

John Buckner, Assignee }
     vs   }
James Devenport   }
                                            [102]

Jury N° 1

We, the Jury, do find for the Plaintiff One hundred and fifty Dollars and Cost of Suit.

The Plaintiff Came forward and Stayed Execution untill the 1st day of March Next.

W. Stephens   John Buckner
Test. Jn° Lumpkin, Clk   Isaac Hodge, F. man

Thursday the 28th of September 1797.

The Honorable Court Adjourned untill Tomorrow 9 O'Clock.

Friday the 29th September 1797

The Court Met According to adjournment. Present, His Honor Judge Stephens.

James Magbee }
    vs   } Case
Jeffrey Early }

Appeal Withdrawn September Term 1797 By James Magbee. Original Verdict Confirmed.

John Griffin   }
Thomas Goodwin}
     vs   } Trover
James Brooks   }

Jury Sworn Nº 1

1. Reubin Embry	5. Miner Johnson	9. James Magbee
2. Edward Prior	6. Abner Aldridge	10. George Varner
3. John Acre	7. Ja^s Devenport	11. Mathew Wiley
4. Benjamin Staton	8. Robert Ellott	12. James Taylor

We find for the Plaintiffs Twenty five Cents, With Cost.

Robert Ellott, Forman

Griffin & Goodwin, Adm^{rs}}   [103]
     vs   } Case Trover Verdict by Consent for Plaintiff
James Brooks   }

The Plaintiff Appears in this Case Without Cost, And the Appeal Not to be Withdrawn, but by Consent of Both parties.

John Michael,   }
Surviving Partner of }
Michael & Sims   }
     vs   } Sheriff's Report on hand Claimed by William Mcelroy
John Mcelrory   }

Witnesses, Richard Bailey, Nathl Bridges.

The Property Claimed by William Mcelrory is four hundred Acres of land Goldengrove Creek Oglethorpe County on Issue Made up.

Jury Sworn

1. James Broton	5. John Wilks	9. William Freman
2. Rush Thornton	6. Thomas Morgin	10. Charles Hardman
3. Henry Hartsfield	7. Jacob Elsburey	11. Henry Bell
4. William Hartsfield	8. Robert Maxfield	12. John Tanner

We, the Jury, find the Property to be held Through fraud and for the Execution to go on.

Charles Hardman, F. man

Cartwright }
    vs   } Sheriff's Report
Epps Tatum }

Fi fa Levied on Negro Henry, Two Cows & Calves, One hiffer, one horse, & Ten Bussels of Corn. Claimed by Howell Tatum. Issue Made up.

Same Jury N° 1 as in Brookses Case, Except Edward Prior Challenged and Middleton Brooks Sworn in his place.

Witnesses Sworn, Henry Haynes, John Shropshire, Jeremiah Wooton, Edward Prior, John Brookes.

We, of the Jury, do find the property to be Epps Tatum's and do Assess Damage against the Claimmint for Thirty dollars, With Cost of Suit.

Robert Ellott, Forman

The Grand Jury Brought in the following Bills (to Wit).   [104]

The State }
    vs   } Ind^t Assault
Howell Tatum }

True Bill.   James Thomas, F. man

The State }
    vs   } Ind^t Assault
Ephraim Phair }

True Bill.   James Thomas, F. man

The State }
    vs   } Ind^t Trespass
Alaxander Mccune }

True Bill.   James Thomas, F. man

The State }
  vs   } Ind^t Selling Liquor Without Licence
William Ragsdale }

True Bill.   James Thomas, F. man

The State }
  vs   } Ind^t Selling Liquor Without Licence
Henry Bell }

True Bill.   James Thomas, F. man

The State }
  vs   } Ind^t Murder
Nancy Warters }

No Bill.   James Thomas, F. man

James Taylor }
  vs   } Case
John Eakols & }
Christopher Irvin }

We do Confess Judgment for the Sum of One hundred and Seven dollars &
fourteen Cents, With Interest and Cost of Suit, Execution to be Stayed until
Christmast Next.

Test. Jno Lumpkin, Clk   Christopher Irvin
                                            John Eakols

The State }   [105]
  vs   }
Howell Tatum }

I, Howell Tatum, and I, John Garrott, Acknowledge Ourselves Justly Indebted to
his Excellency the Governor, for the Time being, in the Sum of Three hundred
Dollars, that is to Say, Said Tatum in the Sum of Two hundred dollars and the
Security in the Sum of One hundred dollars, Conditioned if the Above Howell
Tatum Shall well And Truly Appear at the Next Superior Court to be held in and
for the County of Oglethorpe on the Twenty Eight day of March Next and not

90

Depart Therefrom Without leave of the Court, then the Above Obligation to be Void, Otherwise to remain in full force and Virtue.

Test. Jn° Lumpkin, Clk   H. Tatum
                                                John Garrott

                                                Wm Stephens

The Honorable Court Adjourned untill Tomorrow Nine O'Clock Saturday the 30th day of September 1797.

The Court Met According to Adjournment. Present, His Honor Judge Stephens.

Christopher Orr }
        vs   } September Term 1797
Joseph Wilson   }

Illegallity of Execution to proced, Deducting Two dollars Eighty Seven & half Cents from the Witnesses Cost.

The State   }
        vs   }
Samuel Smith   }
Elizabeth Smith }
Charrity Swan   }
William Warters }
Joseph Warters   }
Ann Warters   }
Charity Bennett }

Samuel Smith, Elizabeth Smith, Charity Swan, William Warters, Joseph Warters, Ann Warters, Charity Bennett Being Sollemly Caled to Appear and give Evidence against Nancy Warters for the Murder of her Child and Not Appearing.

Upon Motion of the Solicitor General, Ordered that the recognizance be Estraited. Sire facius Ordered.

The State   }
     vs   }
Godfrey Addams }
Allen Kelough   }
Robert Campell }

Godfrey Addams, the Principal, being Sollemly Caled Caled an Allen Kelough & Robert Campell, His Securities, & they Not Appearing, upon Motion of The Solicitor General, Ordered that the Recognizance be Estraited.

On Motion of Samuel Knox and Others, for a Writ of Partition to divide the real Estate of Absolum Knox, Dec[d], it is Ordered that a Writ of Partition do Issue in the Terms of the Stattute, and Eleven Discreat persons Named As Partitioners, And that Each party be Notified that they may be Apprised thereof.

William Stephens
30th September 1797

Richard Smith, ex dem   }
Charles Finch   }
       vs   } Ejectment
Joseph Rachford & Others }

Jury Sworn N° 1

1. John Porter
2. Robert Ellott
3. John Acre
4. James Kenney
5. Isaac Hodge
6. James Taylor
7. Jacob Elsbury
8. Patrick Brewer
9. Burwell Brewer
10. Laurence Kennebrew
11. Richard Thornton
12. Middleton Brooks

We, the Jury, find for the Plaintiff all the land within the Boundaries of his grant, With Cost of Suit.

John Porter, F. man

John Towns   }
     vs   } Deceit
Harrason Musgrove }

The Same Jury as Above.

We, the Jury, find for the plaintiff Two hundred Eighty One Dollars, With Cost, With Stay of Execution untill the first day of March 1798.

John Porter, F. man

John Smith   }   [107]
Assignee of   }
Thomas Carter   }
    vs   }
Humphrey Edmonson }

Jury N° 1

We find for the Plaintiff forty five dollars, With Interest from the 26th of December 1796 and Cost of Suit.

John Porter, F. man

The State   }
    vs   } Ind^t Selling Liquor Without Licence
James Kenney   }

The Defendant having Plead guilty and the Offenc being Charged to have been Commited Since the Passing of the Act Altering the rates of Coin, it is Ordered that the defendant be fined in the Sum of Ten pounds, Payable in Dollars at four Shillings & Eight pence Each Equal to the Sum of Twenty four Dollars.

Laurence Kennebrew }
         vs   } Case
Shadrick Kennebrew }

Same Jury as Above, Except John Smith in place of Laurence Kenebrew.

We find for the Plaintiff forty Seven Dollars & Cost of Suit.

John Porter, F. man

The State }
    vs   } Ind^t Seling Liquors Without Licence
Henry Bell}

Henry Bell Came into Open Court and bound himself in the Sum of Two hundred dollars and William Walker in the Sum of One hundred dollars, to his Excellency and his Successors in Office.

The Condition of the Recognizance is Such that, if the Above Bound Henry Bell Shall personally Appear at the Next Superior Court, then and there to Answer to a Bill of Indictment for Seling liquor Without license, then the recognizance to be Void, Else to remain in full force and Virtue. Sep^t 30th 1797

Test. Jno Lumpkin, Clk   Henry Bell
                                             William Walker

The State   }   [108]
     vs   } Ind^t Assault
Miligin Patrick }

True Bill.   James Thomas, F. man

The Grand Jury Brought in their presentments, Which were read and Ordered to be filed, there being no further Business for the Grand Jury, they were dismised With Thanks. The Pettit Jury were also discharged.

                                             William Stephens

Benjamin Bustin }
     vs   } Case
John Moore   }

I, the Defendant, and we, Permenus Haynes & Andrew Bell, Acknowledge Ourselves Jointly & Severally Bound to the Plaintiff in the Sum mentioned in the Bail Bond, on the Condition that, if the Defendant Shall be Cast in his Suit, we will pay the Condemnation money, or Surrender himself as the law Directs, or we will do it for him. Taken and Acknowledged in Open Court.

Test. Jno Lumpkin, Clk   Permenus Haynes
                                             A. Bell

                                             W. Stephens

The Honorable Court then Adjourned untill Monday Nine O'Clock.

Monday the 2nd day of October 1797. The Honorable the Court Met According to Adjournment. Present, His Honor Judge Stephens.

The State   }   [109]
    vs   } Ind^t Seling Liquors Without Licence
William Ragsdale}

William Ragsdale came into Court and Acknowledged himself bound to his Excellency Governor in the Sum of Two hundred Dollars and Howell Tatum, as Security, in the Sum of One hundred dollars, the Condition of the Above Obligation is Such that, if the Above William Ragsdale Shall well and Truly Appear at the Next Superior Court to be held in and for the County of Oglethorpe on the Twenty Eighth day of March Next to Answer to a bill of Indictment perfered Against him for Seling Liquors Without Licence, then the Above Obligation to be Void, Else to remain in full force and Virtue.

Test. Jno Lumpkin, Clk   Wm Ragsdale
                                 Howell Tatum

Powell }
   vs } on the report of the register of Probates About a will &c
Powell }

On Reading the report of the Register in this Case and the Issue made up, it is Ordered that, as the Will Appears Prima Facia to be Legal, the Exo^{rs} will be Considered in possession of the Effects of the dec^d, in the mean time, let a Commission to Exammine Witnesses on Interrogatories in Virginia, or Elsewhere, Agreeable to the Common usage and practice in Similar Cases.

                             Wm Stephens
                             2 October 1797

Ordered, that all Grand and pettit Jurors be fined except Sufficient Excuses be filed as the Law directs.

That the presentments of the Grand Jury and Charge of the Judge be   [110] Carefully Entered upon the Minutes and Both Published as requested by the Grand Jury.

Doe, on the Demise }
of Brown   }
    vs   } Ejectment
Weaver   }

Declaration Amended by Ading Anthony Henry, in right of his wife, Elizabeth Brown, and a rule of Survey Ordered by Consent and filed.

On Motion, it is Ordered that Burwell Brown be discharged from his Recognizance.

Grand Jurors for Next Term (Viz.)

1. Josiah Hailes
2. John Sankey
3. Thomas Hendon
4. Glen Owen
5. William McCree
6. John Gresham, Sen[r]
7. John Embry
8. Abel Gower
9. William Hitchcock
10. Thomas Simonton
11. Benjamin Baldwin
12. William Sharp
13. James Daniel
14. John Cargile
15, William Strong
16. John Hardin
17. William Mathews
18. James Daniel, Jun[r]
19. Guy Smith
20. William Bledsoe
21. Francis Mereweather
22. Thomas Dunn
23. Nicholas Hopson

Pettit Jurors for Next Term

1. Robert Gresham
2. Burdit Finch
3. W[m] Johnson
4. David Ray
5. Job Callaway
6. Hen Stringfellow
7. Zac Wilson
8. John Johnson
9. Nathan Adkinson
10. John Powell
11. Thomas Brown
12. Hugh Freman
13. John Rutledge
14. Blake Carter
15. Solomon Jinnings
16. William Golsbey
17. Thomas Gill
18. Jessee Mcintosh
19. Robert Tuggle
20. Theophiles Hill
21. John McClane
22. Thomas Lee

23. Joseph Beavers
24. John Lumberton[blot]
25. David Glaze
26. William Bowls
27. Joseph Rodgers
28. John Gibney
29. Ben[j] Stovall
31. John Starkey
32. Nathan Wingfield
33. John Kidd
34. James Hinis
35. Thomas Adkinson
36. John Lumpkin
37. Sam[l] Northington
40. W[m] Ealey   [111]
41. John Luckey
42. Josiah Carr
43. Phil Edmonson
44. Jessee Ealy
45. Joseph Dun
46. Shelton Standerpe

96

| 30. Harris Gresham | 38. Robert Beasley | 47. Walter Maxey |
| | 39. Charles Burk, Jun[r] | 48. John Mcguire |

The Court Adjourned to the Next Term.

W. Stephens

Charge of Judge Stephens }
To the Grand Jury of   }
Oglethorpe County   }
September Term 1797   } Gentlemen of the Grand Jury

It is Now to be understood that Society Being formed For the benefit of Mankind and for there Security and hapiness, that Natural and State Government have been Erected, the formar Intended for Our Common welfare United people, As Such we are bound to Support that Natural Consequence by A Due Observance of its Constitutions and Laws free from prejudice or foreign Influence of Any kind.

We are Equally, if Not more perticularly, Interested in Our State Government and its Nessessary Regulations, and in this the People will find the propriety of Laying Such a foundation for good Government in the Choice of Independant honest men, Whose Carracters and Abilities go hand in hand, free from Partial Views, and Whose Object is the publick good. Citizens of this Description being So Intitled will Allways Receive the Countenance and Sufferages of there fellow Citizens.

The [blot]   [112]
And in this as being Nearest at home being Doubtless the Greatest, Care will be Taken As to those Appointments. When You inquire into greavences that Exist, You will Make them known by Presentments founded only on the Truth of fact. Amongst the Evils that are prevalant, I find None of More pernitious Tendency than that of Slander, Either by words or Scandelous And libellious publickations. While this Mischievious practice is Countenanced in Either way, no person's reputation is Safe from Such Malitious Attacks and it is Extremely Injurious from the Dificulty that Accrus in punishing the Transgreser, those persons that Are guilty of this Offence and Shew there fondness for Whispering Away the Carrecters of there Neighbours Are great Enemies to Society And Deserve Severe Reprehention. On Deliberating on Cases before you, let me Urge to you the Greatest Caution, free from Prejudice on the One hand, and Equally so from fear on the Other hand, Exammine with the highest Circumspection the Witnesses that Come before you, and After well weighing there Testimoney, then Determine Accordingly. I Need Not Urge to you how Nessacery it is for All your Citizens

97

to Support the Laws, Establish good Order, And uphold the weak from the Opprestion. And this is probably more perticularly Expected from those in Elevated Situation and in respectable Officeses. Amongst the greatest of your Obligations, Gentlemen, there are None more Important than a due Attention to and respect for Religion, the Establishments of Religious rights

With good Morrals Are strong Amounts of a Society   [113]
[blot]
and prepare there minds for future hapiness that may result from principels of Such permenency that Cannot be Shaken. The Court Will be ready at All Times to give you Such Assistance as the Nature of the Cases may Require. And you may Depend, Gentlemen, that no unnessasary Delay Will be Admited to keep you Impropely from your Pursuits.

State of Georgia   }
Oglethorpe County } September Term 1797

We, the Grand Jury for the County of Oglethorpe, Do on Our Oaths make the Following presentments. (To Wit)

Miles Jinning for Seling Spirituous Liquors Without Licence in Smaller Quantities than One Quart.

Joseph Beavers for Seling Spirituous Liquors in Smaller Quantities than One Quart Without Licence.

Thomas Watts for Seling Spirituous Liquors in Smaller Quantities than One Quart Without Licence.

We Present as a greavance that the Malitia Are Not paid for Services Rendered to the State.

Greaving With Deep Concern an Act of the Congress of the United States of America laying Duties on Stamped Vellum parchment and paper as pregnant with may and great Inconveniences, Respectfully beg leave to recommend to Our Next Legislature by remonstrance & instructions to Our members in Congress to have the Same Repealed.

We Return our thanks to his Honor Judge Stephens for his Juditious   [114]
Charge at the Commencement of and perticular Attention During the Term to the

duties of his High Office And beg That his honor's Charge, Together with These Our presentments be published in the State's Gazette.

James Thomas, F. man	John Marks
Thomas Johnson	Ezekel Gillum
John Moore	Andrew Bell
William Hendon	Permenus Haynes
Robert Haynes	Robert Beavers
Richard Goolsbey	Thomas Scoggin
John Fluker	Clifton Woodroof
Osnan Whatley	John Garrott
James Rutledge	James Devenport
John Ramsey	

Laurence Kenebrew}
    vs   }
Shadrick Kenebrew }

Shadrick Kenebrew Came forward and George Varner, his Security, Within the four Days, And Acknowledged themselves Indebted Jointly And Severally in the Sum of Two hundred Dollars, or pay the Eventual Condemnation money for the Stay of Execution Sixty Days. Acknowledged this 4th day of October 1797.

Test. Jn° Lumpkin, Clk   Shadrick Kenebrew
                          George Varner

John Smith, Assignee }
of Thomas Carter   }
     vs   }
Humphrey Edmonson }

Humphrey Edmonson, being Dissatisfied With the Judgment in the Above Case, prays an Appeal to a Special Jury, With Robert Haynes Security, and binds them Selves to pay the Eventual Condemantion money or to Surrender the principal in Execution. Octr 5th 1797

Test. Jn° Lumpkin, Clk   Humphrey Edmonson
                          Robert Haynes

Richard Smith, ex dem }   [115]
Charles Finch   }
        vs   } Ejectment
Joseph Rachford &   }
Harmon Holt   }

Joseph Rachford, being Dissatisfied ~~in the Above Case~~ With the Judgment In the
Above Case, prayed an Appeal to a Special Jury, With Robert Thomson Security,
and binds themselves to pay the Eventual Condemnation money or to Surrender
the principal in Execution. Octr 5th 1797

Test. Jno Lumpkin, Clk   Joseph Ratchford
                                             Robert Thomson

At a Superior Court Begun and held for the County of Oglethorpe on the 28th day
of March 1798. Present, His Honor Thomas P. Carnes.

The Commission of his honor the Judge and the Clause of the Juditiary Act,
Which Directs the Judge to Alternate and being read, Ordered that the Venerery
of the Grand and Pettit Jury Over When the Jury Appeared. (Viz)

Grand Jurors

1. Wm Mathews   9. William Strong   16. James Freman
2. Thos Hendon   10. John Hardin   17. Barnard Smith
3. Glen Own   11. William Walker   18. John Luckie
4. William McCree   12. Guy Smith   19. James Daniel, Junr
5. John Embry   13. Thomas Simonton   20. William Bledsoe
6. Abel Gower   14. William M. Stokes
7. William Hickcock   15. John Cargile
8. William Sharp

Elijah Christian }   [116]
        vs   }
John Moore   }

Continued by Consent of Parties.

James Edwards }
Assignee of Salmon}
  vs   }
Spencer Reynolds }

I, the Defendant, and I, William Strother, Acknowledge Ourselves Jointly and Severally Bound to the Plaintiff in the Sum mentioned in the Bail Bond on the Condition that, if the Defendant fails, we will pay the Eventual Condemnation money, or Surrender himself as the Law Directs, or we will do it for him. Taken in Open Court.

Test. Jn° Lumpkin, Clk   Spencer Reynolds
            William Strother

Benjamin Bustin }
  vs   } Debt
John Moore }

I do hereby Confess Judgment for the Sum of five hundred Dollars, with five per Cent Interest from the first Day of March one Thousand Seven hundred and Ninety Six, with Stay of Execution untill the first Day of March Next, provided that within five Days William Harvie be Given as Security for the payment thereof. March 28 1798

Jn° Walton   John Moore

Benjamin Bustin }
  vs   } Debt
John Moore }

I do hereby Confess Judgment for the Sum of five hundred Dollars, with five per Cent Interest from the first Day of March one Thousand Seven hundred and Ninety Six. I, William Harvie, do Acknowledge myself Jointly Bound with the Defendant, John Moore, for the payment of the principal, Interest, and Cost of the Judgment in this Case.

Test. Jn° Lumpkin, Clk   W. Harvie

John Williamson }
    vs   }
Joseph Wilson   }

I, the Defendant, and I, Jesse Willingham, Acknowledge Ouselves Jointly and Severally Bound to the Plaintiff in the Sum mentioned in the bail bond on the Condition that the Defendant fails, we will pay the Eventual Condemnation money, or Surrender himself as the Law Directs, or we will Do it for him. Taken and Acknowledged in Open Court.

Test. Jn° Lumpkin, Clk   Joseph Wilson
                                  Jessee Willingham

Major Wilcox   }
    vs   }
Alaxander Gordon }

I do hereby Confess Judgment for the Sum of Two hundred and Twenty Two Dollars Sixty Nine and a half Cents, with Interest from the Tenth day of December One Thousand Seven hundred and Ninety Two untill paid, With Stay of Execution four months.

Test. Robert Walker   Alaxander Gordon

James Hamble }
    vs   }
John Wilks   }

I, the Defendant, and I, Benjamin Wilks, Acknowledge Ouselves Jointly And Severally Bound to the Plaintiff in the Sum mentioned in the Bail Bond on the Condition that the Defendant fails, we will pay the Eventual Condemnation money, or Surrender himself as the Law Directs, or I will Do it for him. Taken and Acknowledged in Open Court.

Test. Jn° Lumpkin, Clk   John Wilks
                                  Benjamin Wilks

James B[smear] }
    vs   }
James Stovall   }

I, Dasher Bragg, Acknowledge Acknowledge myself Justly Indebted to the Plaintiff the Sum Mentioned in the bail Bond, on the Condition that the Defendant fails, ~~we~~ I will pay the Eventual Condemnation Money, or Surrender himself as the Law Directs, or I will do it for him. Taken and Acknowledged in Open Court.

Test. Jn° Lumpkin, Clk   Dasher Bragg

William Hay }
     vs   }
Ge° Lumpkin }

Death of the Plaintiff Suggested & Gilbert Hay, Charles Hay, & James Hay, Executors, made parties to the record. Continued.

Douglas Watson and   }
Elizabeth Thornton,   }
Exo^{rs} of Joshua Thornton }
        vs   }
Alaxander Joyce   }
Joshua Askew   }

Death of Douglas Watson Suggested. Ordered, that the Suit Progress in the Name of the Surviving Exo^{rs} and the writ Amended in that regard. Continued.

Ben^j Baldwin &   }
Douglas Watson   }
     vs   }
Nathaniel Durkee & }
Cudberth Coleman }

Death of Douglas Watson Suggested. Ordered, that the Suit progress in the Name of the Surviving Exo^{rs} and the Writ amended in that regard. Continued.

The Honorable the Court Adjourned untill Tomorrow Nine O'Clock.

                       Thos P. Carnes

The Honorable Court Met According to Adjournment March 29 1798.   [119]
Present, His Honor Judge Carnes.

Peter Hoof   }
     vs   }
John Franks &   }
Nath¹ Bradford }

I, the Defendant, Nathaniel Bradford, and I, Lewis Pope, Acknowledge Ourselves Jointly and Severally Bound in the Sum Mentioned in the Bail Bond, on the Condition that the Defendant fails, we will pay the Eventual Condemnation Money for him, or Surrender himself as the Law Directs, or we will do it for him. Taken and Acknowledged in Open Court.

Test. Jnº Lumpkin, Clk   N. Bradford
                                           Lewis Pope

John Williams   }
     vs   }
Pechee Bledsoe &   }
Joseph Wilson   }

I, the Defendant Joseph Wilson, And I, John Legit, Acknowledge Ourselves Jointly and Severaly Indebted to the Plaintiff the Sum Mentioned in the Bail bond, on the Condition that the Defendant fails, we will pay the Eventual Condemnation Money for him, or Surrender himself as the Law Directs, or we will do it for him. Taken and Acknowledged in Open Court.

Test. Jnº Lumpkin, Clk   Joˢ Wilson
                                           Jnº ꝯ L Legit, his mark

Jacob Elsbury }
     vs   }
John Wilks   }

Setled at plaintiff's Cost.

Jacob Elsbury }   [120]
     vs   }
John Wilks   }

104

Setled at Plaintiff's Cost.

John Wilks   }
    vs   }
Jacob Elsbury }

Setled at Plaintiff's Cost.

Gerard Banks   }
    vs   }
John Gresham & }
David Creswell }

Jury Sworn N° 2

1. Jn° Kidd   5. Wm Johnson   9. William Doggit
2. Bailey George   6. Cudberth Collier   10. Wm Ragsdell
3. Charles Burk   7. Ephraim Jackson   11. Jessee Clay
4. Thomas Good   8. Lemuel Black   12. Permenus Haynes

We Find for the Plaintiff five hundred and Twenty five Dollars and Twenty five Cents & Cost of Suit.

Permenus Haynes, F. man

Robert Flournoy }
    vs   }
Charles Burk   }

Jury Sworn N° 1

1. Wm Johnson   5. Joseph Rogers   9. Josiah Carr
2. Job Calaway   6. James Hines   10. Jessee Ealey
3. Zac Wilson   7. Charles Burk   11. Thomas Brown
4. John Powell   8. William Ealy   12. Walter Maxey

We find for the Plaintoff One hundred Dollars and Eighty Eight Cents, With Cost of Suit.

Jn° Powell, F. man

The State   }
    vs   } Ind^t Riot
Robert Lumpkin }
Harroson Lumpkin }
& John Lumpkin }

True Bill.   William Mathews, F. man

The State   }   [121]
    vs   } Ind^t Assault
Joseph McElrory }

True Bill.   William Mathews, F. man

The State   }
    vs   } Ind^t Assault
Lewis McElrory }

True Bill.   William Mathews, F. man

The State   }
    vs   } Ind^t Assault
Joseph Wilson }

No Bill.   Wm Mathews, F. man

Amos Wilks }
And Others   }
    vs   }
Thomas Good }
& Others   }

It is Mutually Agreed between the parties to Submit all matters in dispute to the artbitrament & award of Burwell Pope & John Lumpkin, Esquires, With the power of umpirage, Whose award Shall be final and Conclusive and Considered as the Judgment of the Court & the Arbitrators, on giving Ten days notice to Each party, may meet at Lexington in the County of Oglethorpe at any time, Between Now and the Next Term, Whose award Shall be returned at the Next Term.

Nathaniel Willis, Plff^s Att^y
P. Allin, Def^{ds} Att^y

The State }
    vs } Ind^t Assault
Abel Penington }

True Bill.   Wm Mathews, F. man

The State }
    vs } Ind^t Libel
John Shropshire }

No Bill.   Wm Mathews, F. man

Richard Smith }   [122]
& R. McAlpin }
    vs } Ejectment
William Stiles & }
William Edwards }

On Motion of Counsel for the Defendant, it is Ordered that a Survey be Made by the County Surveyor of the premises in Dispute between the Above parties and that Said Surveyor do return to the Next Superior Court a full and Compleat plat of Both the Surveys under Which the Said parties Claim, Designating perticularly how and Where the lines of Said Surveys Interfears With Each Other & That Ten Days Previous Notice be given to the Opisite parties of the Time of making Such Surveys.

James Mathews }
    vs }
William Arther & }
Jeffrey Early }

Jury Nº 1.

We find for the Plaintiff One hundred and four Dollars & Twenty Eight Cents & Cost of Suit.

Jnº Powell, F. man

Execution Not to Issue till After five months from the date of Verdict.

J. Griffin, Plff⁵ Attʸ

Nathaniel Bullock }
    vs   } Case
John Fluker   }

Jury Nº 2.

We, the Jury, find for the Plaintiff, after Reducting the prising, One hundred dollars, With Cost of Suit.

Permenus Haynes, F.

The State   }   [123]
    vs   } Indᵗ Assault
Robert Kenney }

True Bill.   Wᵐ Mathews, F. man

John Denn, dem   }
The Heirs & Representatives }
of Greenbury Lee, Decᵈ   }
        vs   }
Richard Fenn &   }
William Beasley   }

On Motion of Council for Plaintiff, it is Ordered that the Surveyor for the County of Oglethorpe do make a resurvey of the lines of Both the Surveys under which the Above Parties Claims & do return a Plat of the Same to the Clerk's Office on or before the Next Superior Court Disignating in Said Plat how and Where the lines of Said Surveys do Interfere and that Ten days previous Notice of Such Reservey be given to the Defendant.

Charles Daniel }
    vs   } Ejectment
Joshua Glass }

On Motion, it is Ordered that William Baldwin, Aron Parks & Ann his Wife, late Ann Baldwin, Ephraim Baldwin, & Owen Baldwin, Heirs of David Baldwin, be Admited Defendants in Lieu of Said Glass upon the usual Terms.

The State   }
    vs   } Assault
Milican Patrick}

The prisoner Came and delivered himself to the Court & was discharged by his Honor Judge Carnes.

William Penworth   }   [124]
Demise of Anthony Haney }
And Others   }
       vs   } Trespass Ejectment
John Doe & David Weaver }

On Motion of Councel in behalf of the Defendant, it is Ordered that the County Surveyor do make a Survey of the premises in dispute Designating therein perticularly the lines of Each Survey and pointing Out how they Interfere and that he report to the Next Superior Court to be held in and for the County of Oglethorpe how he Shall have Executed the Same, and that Ten days Notice of the time of Executing Such Survey be given to the Oppisite party.

The State   }
    vs   } Ind^t Assault
Joseph Mcelrory}

The State   }
    vs   } Ind^t Assault
Lewis Mcelroy }

We, Joseph Mcelrory & Lewis Mcelroy, and we Jacob Mcelrory & Mary Mcelrory, Acknowledge Ourselves Jointly and Severally bound to his Excellency the Governor, for the time being, or his Successors in office, the Sum of Six hundred dollars, that is to Say, Jo^s & Lewis in the Sum of Two hundred Dollars Each and Jacob & Mary in the Sum of One hundred dollars Each.

Conditioned that, if the Said Joseph & Lewis Mcelroys Shall appear at the Next Superior Court to be held for the County of Oglethorpe on the Twenty Eighth day of Septr Next & do not Depart the Said Court Without leave, then the Above Obligation to be Void, or Else to remain in full force & Virtue. Taken & Acknowledged in open Court.

Test. Jno Lumpkin, Clk

Joseph Mcelrory
Lewis X Mcelrory, his mark
Jacob Mcelrory
Mary I Mcelrory, her mark

The State   }
    vs   } Ind^t Assault   [125]
Howell Tatum }

True Bill.   James Thomas, F. man

George Mathews, Junr, Esquire, having made Application to be admitted to the practice as an Attorney, Solicitor, & proctor of the Several Courts of law and Equity Within this State, and the Said George Mathews having undergone the usial Exammination, and being found to possess Competent Knowledge, he Appeared in Open Court and Took the usial Oath.

Whereupon, Ordered that the Name of the Said George Mathews be entered on the rool of Attorneys, And that he be permited to practice accordingly.

The State   }
    vs   } Ind^t Assault
Howell Tatum }

Jury Sworn

1. Wm Johnson   5. Joseph Rogers   9. Josiah Carr
2. Job Calaway   6. James Hinens   10. Jessee Ealey

| 3. Zach Wilson | 7. Charles Burk | 11. Thomas Brown |
| 4. John Powell | 8. William Ealy | 12. Walter Maxey |

Who Returned the following Verdict.

The Court having Considered this Case, Ordered that Howell Tatum pay a fine of five dollars and Cost of Prosecution & be therafter discharged. Cost paid.

Nathaniel Bullock }   [126]
     vs   }
John Fluker   }

John Fluker, the Defendant, being dissatisfied with the Judgment in the above Case, has entered an Appeal to a Special Jury, With Pechee Bledsoe Security, and Bind themselves to pay the Eventual Condemnation money or Suurender the principle in discharge. Taken and Acknowledged the 29th day of March 1798.

Test. Jno Lumpkin, Clk   John Fluker
                                   Pechy Bledsoe

Robert Flournoy }
     vs   }
Charles Burk   }

Charles Burk, being dissatisfied With the Judgment in the Above Case, has Entered an Appeal to a Special Jury, With Charles Burk, Junr Security, and bind themselves to pay the Eventual Condemnation money or Surrender the principal in discharge. March 29th 1798

Test. Jno Lumpkin, Clk   Charles Burk, Senr
                                   Charles Burk, Junr

The State   }
     vs   } Ind^t Assault
John Lumpkin, Junr }

We, John Lumpkin and Absolum Hendrick Acknowledge Ourselves Jointly and Severally Bound to his Excellency, or his Successors in Office, the Sum of three hundred Dollars, that is to Say,

John Lumpkin in the Sum of Two hundred dollars & the Security One   [127]
hundred dollars.

Conditioned that, if the Said John Lumpkin Shall Appear at the Next Superior
Court to be held in and for the County of Oglethorpe on the Twenty Eighth day
of September Next and Not Depart the Court without leave, then the Above
Obligation to be Void, Otherwise to remain in full force and Virtue. Taken and
Acknowledged in Open Court.

Test. Jnᵒ Lumpkin, Clk   Jnᵒ X Lumpkin, his mark
                                           Absolum Hendrick

John Farson }
    vs   }
Hugh Freman }

Upon the Petition of John Farson praying foreclosure of a Tract of land Containing
Two hundred Acres, lying, Situate, and being in the County of Oglethorpe, on
Cloud Creek in the State of Georgia, on Motion of Mʳ Martin, Attorney for
plaintiff, it is Ordered that the principal, Interest, & Cost be paid upon the Said
Obligation & Morgage to the Court Within Twelve months from the date, and
unless the Same Shall So be paid, & the Equity of redemption Will from thence
forth be foreclosed & Other Proceedings Take place persuent to an Act of
Assembly in Such Case made and provided, pased on the Ninth Day of December
1790, & it is further Ordered, in persuance of Said Act, that this rule be published
in one of the Publick Gazatts or Served on the Mortgagor, or his Attorney, at least
Nine Months previous to the Time by Which the money Must be paid into Court
as Aforesaid.

The State   }   [128]
    vs   } Indᵗ Trespass
Alaxander McCune }

The State   }
    vs   } Indᵗ Trespass
Ephraim Phair }

In the Above Cases, the Defendants were ready & Moved for Trial, the State
Officer Not being ready. Mʳ Griffin, Counsel for the Defendants, Then Stated to
the Court that the Defendants had Attended and a Witness Material Who resided
Out of the ~~Stat~~ County at a distance, and Moved the Court for an Order to Take

the Exammination of the Said Witness by Interrogatories, the Court Denied the power but With the Consent of the Solicitor Gen[l], Who refusing to give Such Consent, the Causes were Continued to the Next Term.

March Term 1798

The Grand Jury made The following presentments.

We, The Grand Inquest for the County of Oglethorpe, Upon Our Oaths present as Greavances the want of a Bridge over the Dry fork of Long Creek, where the road Croses, leading from Lexington to Washington. Secondly, the want of a road from Lexington to Barber's Bridge on long Creek. Thirdly, that A Number of the Surveyors of roads in this County

have Neglected there duty, so that the roads under there Directions is   [129] Not kept in repair. Fourthly, we Return Our thanks to his honor the Judge for his Juditious Charge to us And his perticular Attention to his duty during the Term & request that his Charge, Together With These Our presentments, be published in the State Gazatte.

William Mathews, Forman

Tho[s] Hendon	Guy Smith
Glenn Owen	Thomas Simonton
W[m] McCree	Addon Simmons
John Embry	W[m] M. Stokes
Abel Gower	James Freman
W[m] Hitchcock	Barnard Smith
W[m] Sharp	John Sankey
W[m] Strong	James Daniel, Jun[r]
John Hardin	W[m] Bledsoe
W[m] Walker	John Cargile

John Christian }
      vs   }
Jn[o] Moore, Esq[r] }

Continued by Consent.

Richard Smith, ex dem }
Jeffrey Early   }
         vs   }
Isaac Holeman &   }
Andrew Pickins   }

Continued by Consent.

William Hay   }   [130]
         vs   }
George Lumpkin }

Death of the plaintiff Suggested. Gilbert Hay, Charles Hay, & James Hay, Exo[rs]
made parties to the record. Continued.

Richard Smith & }
Robert McAlpin   }
         vs   }
William Stiles & }
William Edwards }

A rule of Survey & C[s] Addam Simmons, Defendant, rule of Survey Ordered on
Application of Defendant.

29th day of March 1798

Douglas Watson & }
Elizabeth Thornton }
Exo[rs] of Joshua   }
Thornton, Dec[d]   }
         vs   }
Alaxander Joyce & }
Joshua Askew   }

Death of Douglas Watson Suggested. Ordered, that the Suit progress in the Name
of the Surviving Executrix and the Writ amended in that regard by Consent.
Continued till Next Term.

Robert Flournoy }
         vs   }
Charles Burk   }

March Term 1798.

Orders, Take Verdict for plaintiff for $100.88 Cents.

Samuel Patton }
    vs   }
Lemuel Black }

Continued on Defendant's Affidavit.

Jacob Elsbury }
    vs   }
John Wilks   }

Setled at Plaintiff's Cost.

Jacob Elsbury }
    vs   }
John Wilks   }

Setled at plaintiff's Cost.

Howell Tatum   }
    vs   }
John Dimond & }
Ben^j Stringfellow }

Continued by Consent.

Henry D. Downs   }
    vs   }
John Watts &   }
Redmond Thornton }

Continued by Consent, With Liberty to Amend the Writ.

Jessee Thomson }
    vs   }
William Walker }

Nonsuit.

[131]

John Wilks   }
   vs   }
Jacob Elsbury }

Setled at Plaintiff's Cost.

John Dunn, ex dem   }
Heirs & Representatives }
of Greenbury Lee   }
     vs   }
Richard Fenn &   }
William Beasly   }

Continued by Consent. Rule of Survey Ordered 29th of March 1798.

Benjamin Baldwin }   [132]
& Douglas Watson }
    vs   }
Nathaniel Durkie & }
Cudberth Coleman }

Death of Douglas Watson Suggested. Ordered, that the Suit progress in the Name of the Surviving Exoʳˢ And the Writ be Amended So as to fit the Situation of the Case as to proper parties.

Thoˢ P. Carnes

The Court Then Adjourned till Tomorrow 9 O'Clock.

The Court Met According to Adjournment. Present, His Honor Thomas P. Carnes.

Ordered, that a Certified Copy of Such of the presentments of the Grand Jury as relate to roads and Bridges be Delivered to the Inferior Court, that the Intentions of the Grand Jury may be Carried into full Effect, and that the presentments of the Grand Jury, Together with the Charge of the Judge be published in the State Gazatte, Agreeable to the request of that Body.

The folllowing Persons were drawn to Serve as Grand and Pettit Jurors at the Next Term.

Grand Jurors [133]

1. Wm Walker
2. James Freman
3. Thomas Gilmor
4. James Bradley
5. Charles Allen
6. Isaac Collier
7. Wm Callahan
8. Charles Hay
9. Noel Thornton
10. Aron Johnson
11. Middleton Brooks
12. Ruebin Glaze
13. Robert Haynes
14. William Stewart
15. John T. Gilmore
16. Joseph Hubard
17. James Parks
18. John Luckie
19. John Devenport
20. John George
21. Thomas Holland
22. William Jinnings
23. William Coldwell
24. George Doggit
25. James Rutledge
26. Permenus Haynes
27. Abram Miles
28. Alax Andrews
29. James Marks
30. Henry Pope

Petit Jurors

1. Wm Beasley
2. Saml Bolling
3. Ben^j Noals
4. Richard Haynes
5. Thos Nelloms
6. Semour Lee
7. Daniel Mcintosh
8. O. Higumbottom
9. Jno Goodman
10. Jacob Sansom
11. Wm Caragan
12. Daniel Jackson
13. Joseph Espey
14. Ja^s Bohanon
15. Noah Hill
16. Ge^o Farer
17. Claburn Barnett
18. Thomas Simpson
19. Moses Watkins
20. Bradford Warters
21. Wm Jackson
22. Wiley Sims
23. Aaron Williams
24. Alax Thompson
25. Charles Gillum
26. Ja^s Thomson
27. Wm Gilbert
28. Ja^s Hay
29. Wm Lorance
30. Peter Smith
31. Moses Williams
32. Allen Prior
33. Joel Forrester
34. Hardy Norris
35. James Price
36. Joshua Jinings
37. Av^t Williams
38. Richard Ward
39. Leo Young
40. Wm Ramsey
41. Robert Holmes
42. Thos Shields
43. Isaac Hodge
44. Ge^o Hudspeth
45. Richard Greer
46. Robert Beasley
47. Joseph Shields
48. Wm Lunsford
49. Mark Sims
50. Val Patton
51. Archer Norris
52. Richard Thornton
53. Thomas Loyd, Junr
54. Ben^j Barnett
55. Josiah Low

Richard Asbury }   [134]
     vs   } Attachment
Henry D. Downs }

Judgment by Default.

Edward Powell, Junr }
     vs   }
Semour Powell   }

Cavat Entered With the Register of Probate's Office of the County by Edward Powell against Semour Powell, Obtaining letters of Administration on the Estate of Edward Powell, Dec^d and on the Register's Report being taken into Consideration by this Court and a Consent being Expressed by the parties that the Court Should deside on the Case Without Argument & Without the Intervention of a Jury, Which the Court was Inclined Should be impanneled to Try the matter of fact, Wheather the Testator was Sane or insane At the time of his Making & Publishing the Will produced, Which was dated on the fourt day of November In the Year of Our Lord One Thousand Seven hundred & Ninety five. It is Considered & hereby declared that, for ought which appears from the Evidence produced, the Said Edward Powell at the time of Signing, Publishing, & Declaring his Said last Will & Testament was of Sufficient mind & memory & thereupon, it is Ordered that the Application to the Register of Probates for Letters of Administration of the Estate of the Said Edward Powell be Dismised & that the Executors Named be permitted to have the Said last will & Testament proven & RecordedAgreeable to Law.

Gentlemen of the Grand Jury   [135]

The Object of Rules for Civil Conduct prescribed by the Legislative Authority of Every Society, which we Call Laws, are Certain Land marks by means whereof Each Individual in the Community is to Square his Actions as the Law Commands what is right & prohibited. What is Improper to be done Each person as he attends to Command of Law or Willfully Conducts himself in Opposition thereto the Catalogue of Crimes Recognized and made punishable by Our Criminal Lode and Such as we know human Creatures are Capable of Committing is of a Size too large for the Rational, Temperate, and Philosophic to look on without Deploreing the Depravity of human nature. we Can amend this Inclination of being Opposed of all Divine & human Institutions by no Other or more Certain means than by Giving Examples of propriety by our Own Deportment and Inflicting punishment with Certainty on those who may be So Vitious as to Transgress a Certain rigid & Seraputous Infliction of punishments ann[blot] by Law to Given Crimes is thought to be the best method of preventing future Commissitions of them, it is therefore Our Indispensible Duty to Weigh well & With Temper all Such Violations of the Law as Come before us & When Convinced of the propriety of Impropriety of Accusations to get with the utmost firmness in holding up to publick Views the Objects Contemplated in Bills or presentments or to Restore (them if the accusation Should be unfounded) to there Relations fa[faint] this & Society unimpeached. this is the Determination Every One Interested with any part in the administration of Justice Ought to maturely form & Religiously Adhere and I am of a

mind Confident in the beleaf that you [smear]   [136]
are from amongst the Best Informed of your County will act up to these Sentiments with the most Scrupolous Exactness. The words of the Oath you have Taken will apply & Serve to Direct you in the part you are to Act and as the Law officers Together with the Court will be happy in Giving you Such Information as you may Require in Discharge of your present Duty, it will be needless to Detail the Several Offences of which you are to Take notice, the wealth of the County and its Remote Situation from advatageous Convenience well agree the necessity of having your publick roads and Bridges in Substantial Repair & Strict Attention to these Objects will add Greatly both to your property & Convenience and Defaulters in that particular your Strictest Annimadversion.

March the 30th 1798 The Honorable the Superior Court Adjourned till Court in Course.

Exd   Ths P. Carnes

Gerard Banks }
    vs }
Jn° Gresham & }
D. Creswell }

We, the Defendants, being Dissatisfied with the Judgment of the Jury in the above Case, Enter an Appeal to a Special Jury. Roderick Easley Came forward and Entered himself Security to pay the Eventual Condemnation Money, or Surrender the defendants in Execution, or I will do it for him. Taken & Acknowledged before

119

this 30th day of March 1798 }   D. Creswell
Test. Jn° Lumpkin, Clk   }   R. Easley

At a Superior Court Begun & held in & for the County of Oglethorpe   [137]
on the 28th day of September 1798. Present, his Honor Judge Mitchell.

Grand Jurors

1. Wm Walker	8. Charles Hay	15. John Davenport
2. James Freeman	9. Noal Thornton	16. John George
3. Thomas Gilmore	10. Middleton Brooks	17. Thomas Holland
4. James Bradley	11. Reuben Glaze	18. Wm Jennings
5. Wm Callahan	12. Robt Haynes	19. George Doggett
6. Charles Allen	13. Jo^s Hubbard	20. James Rutledge
7. Isaac Collier	14. John Luckie	

Pettit Jurors

1. Wm Beasley	8. George Farrow	15. Peter Smith
2. Saml Boling	9. Bradford Waters	16. Joshua Jennings
3. Richard Haynes	10. Wiley Sims	17. Averton Williams
4. Seamour Lee	11. Alex Thompson	18. Leonard Young
5. Wm Cardin	12. Charles Gillam	19. Isaac Hodge
6. Danl Jackson	13. Ja^s Thompson	20. George Hudspeth
7. Ja^s Bohannon	14. Ja^s Hay	21. Joseph Shields
		22. Wm Lunsford
		23. Mark Sims
		24. Richard Thornton

Richard Smith, Ex dem }
Jeffrey Earley   }
          vs   }
Wm Stiles   }
Isaac Holeman &   }
Andrew Pickins   }

Jury Sworn. First Twelve N° 1.

We, the Jury, find for the plaintiff.

Wm Beasley, F. man

120

William Ha[blot] }
    vs   }
George Lumpkin }

Discontinued.

Richard Smith   }
McAlpin   }
    vs   }
William Stiles & }
William Edwards }

Jury Nº 1

We, the Jury, find for the Plaintiff.

Wᵐ Beasley, F. man

State   }
    vs   } Indᵗ Murder
Patton Wise   }
William Johnson {
John Banks   }
Thomas Brooks   }
George Borum & }
Dunston Banks   }

True Bill.   John Davenport, F. man

The State   }
    vs   } Indᵗ Riot
Patton Wise   }
William Johnson {
John Banks   }
Thomas Brooks   }
George Borum & }
Dunston Banks   }

No Bill.   John Davenport, F. man

121

The State   }
    vs   } Ind^t Assault
Dunston Banks }

No Bill.   John Davenport, F. man

The State   }   [139]
    vs   } Ind^t Assault
Patton Wise }

No Bill.   John Davenport, F. man

John B. Parks, Ad^m }
      vs   } Bill in Equity
Josiah Jordan, Ad^m }
& Others   }

On Motion, Ordered that the Defendant do plead, answer, or demur, not demuring Alone, to the Allegations of the Complainant's Bill in four Callender Months from the Expiration of the present Term, or in Default thereof, the allegations of the Said Bill Shall be Taken Pro Confesso.

Howell Tatum   }
     vs   } Case
John Dimond &   }
Benjamin Stringfellow }

We, the Jury, find for the plaintiff Thirty Two Dollars Sixty Eight & one fourth Cents, with Lawfull Interest.

                                              Leo Young, F. man

I, John Dimond, & I, Samuel Gardner, & I, Joseph McCutchin, Acknowledge themselves Justly Indebted to Howell Tatum the above Sum for the Stay of Execution Sixty Days, if he fails to pay the Same, we will do it for him. Acknowledged in Court.

                                              John Dimond
                                              Saml Gardner
                                              Joseph McCutchin

The Court Adjourned untill Tomorrow Ten O'Clock.   [140]

D. B. Mitchell

The Honorable Court Met According to Adjournment September 29th 1798. Present, his Honor Judge Mitchell.

Richard Milear, Assignee }
of Jeffrey Earley   }
            vs   } Case
John Leftwich   }

I do hereby Acknowledge Satisfaction of the plaintiff's Demand.

Earley, Plff^{ts} Att^y

Susannah & Bennet }
Watts, Appellants   }
            vs   } Case
Edward McCoy   }

Appeal Special Jury

1. Wm Walker	5. Charles Allen	9. Noel Thornton
2. James Freeman	6. Wm Callihan	10. Middleton Brooks
3. Thos Gilmore	7. Isaac Collier	11. Reuben Glaze
4. Ja^s Bradley	8. Charles Hay	12. Joseph Hubbard

We, the Jury, find for the appellants.

Thomas Gilmore, F. man

Johnson Strong   }
Appellant   }
            vs   }
Alexander Gordan }
Respondent   }

Appeal Special Jury

Jury Sworn

1. William Walker
2. Ja^s Freeman
3. Thos Gilmore
4. Ja^s Bradley
5. Charles Allen
6. Wm Callihan

7. Isaac Collier
8. Charles Hay
9. Noel Thornton
10. Middleton Brooks
11. Reuben Glaze
12. Joseph Hubbard

We, the Jury, find for the appellant four hundred Dollars, which   [141]
may be Discharged by making a Special Warrantee Title Agreeable to the Grant.

Thomas M. Gilmore, F. man

William Merrit }
Appellant   }
    vs   }
John Blanton   }
Respondent   }

Appeal Special Jury

Jury Sworn

1. William Walker
2. Ja^s Freeman
3. James Bradley
4. Thos Gilmore
5. Charles Allen
6. Wm Callihan

7. Isaac Collier
8. Charles Hay
9. Noel Thornton
10. Middleton Brooks
11. Reuben Glaze
12. Joseph Hubbard

The appeal withdrawn & the Judgment Below Confirmed.

John Gibson   }
Appellant   }
    vs   }
George Dogget &}
Millery Dogget   }
Respondents   }

Appeal Special Jury

Jury Sworn

1. William Walker
2. James Freeman
3. Thomas Gilmore
4. James Bradley
5. Charles Allen
6. William Callihan

7. Isaac Collier
8. Charles Hay
9. Noel Thornton
10. Middleton Brooks
11. Reuben Glaze
12. Joseph Hubbard

We, the Jury, find for the Respondents.

Thomas M. Gilmore, F. man

John Moore }
Appellant }
   vs }
Francis Gordan }
Respondent }

Appeal withdrawn & Judgment Below Confirmed.

John M[smear] }   [142]
Appelant }
   vs }
Howell Jarrett }
Respondant }

Appeal Withdrawn & the Judgment Below Confirmed.

Harriss }
   vs } Caveat
Hughs }

In this Case, by Consent, it is Ordered that Letters of Administration be Granted to Henry Hill.

John Fluker, App[ts] }
   vs }
Nathaniel Bullock, Resp[t] }

We, the Jury, find for the Respondent One hundred & thirty Two Dollars Seventy five Cents.

Thomas M. Gilmore, F. man

D. B. Mitchell

The Honorable Court then Adjourned Untill monday Morning Ten O'Clock.

Monday the 1st of October The Honorable Met According to Adjournment. Present, his Honour Judge Mitchell.

State   }
  vs   } Ind^t Murder
Patton Wise   }
William Johnson {
John Banks   }
Thomas Brooks }
George Borum & }
Dunston Banks }

The prisoners being Brought to the Bar to be Tried, the following Jurors Were Impannelled & Sworn. (To Wit)

1. James Thompson	5. James Colloy	9. Benjamin Barnet [143]
2. Saml Whitehead	6. William Smith	10. William McBride
3. Isam Davis	7. John Hubbard	11. George Hudspeth
4. Smith Gammon	8. Isaiah Goolsby	12. Mark Sims

We, the Jury, find the prisoners not Guilty.

George Hudspeth, F. man

The State }
  vs   } Ind^t Selling Liquor Without License
Edward Prior}

True Bill.   John Davenport, F. man

The Court then Adjourned Untill Tomorrow Ten O'Clock.

D. B. Mitchell

Tuesday the 2nd day of October 1798 The Honorable Court Met According to Adjournment. Present, his Honor Judge Mitchell.

The State }
    vs   } Ind^t Selling Liquor Without License
John Prior }

True Bill.   John Davenport, F. man

The State   }
    vs   } Ind^t Assault
Robert Lumpkin }

True Bill.   John Davenport, F. man

The State   }
    vs   } Ind^t Mahem
William Wimpey }

True Bill.   John Davenport, F. man

James Thomas }   [144]
    vs   } Case
John George   }

On motion of Mr Jones, Counsel for the Defendant, and it appearing that Due notice hath been Given, it is Ordered that, on the Trial of this Cause, the plaintiff, James Thomas, produce a bond Given to him by the Defendant for making Titles to the Land, which is the Subject of the present Action, & which Contains matter pertenent to the Case in question, or Shew good Cause to the Satisfaction of the Court Why he Cannot produce the Same.

John Wray   }
    vs   } fifa Sheriff's Reports
Adm^s of Richard Call }

Thomas Carr   }
        vs   } fifa Sheriff's Reports
Adm^s of Richard Call }

The Claims of Alex Cummins & Humphrey Edmonson withdrawn & that of Joseph Moore Dismised.

Jesse Sanders &   }
Henry Hampton   }
        vs   } Covenant
Ferdinand Phinizy }

Jury Sworn

1. Samuel Boling	5. George Farrow	9. James Say
2. Richard Haynes	6. Bradford Waters	10. Peter Smith
3. Semour Lee	7. Alex Thompson	11. Joshua Jennings
4. Daniel Jackson	8. Charles Gilham	12. Aventon Williams

We, the Jury, find for the Defendant.

George Farrow, F. man

September Term 1798 }   [145]
State of Georgia   }
Oglethorpe County   }   We, the Grand Jury for the County aforesaid, do present as a Greviance that the Commissions Appointed for the promotion of Literature in this County have not done their Duty in Carrying into Effect a Law for that purpose made and Provided.

We also present as a Greviance that a Direct Road Leading from Lexington to the Cider Shoals on the Oconee River have not been Opened Agreeable to an Order of Court for that Purpose.

We present Nicholas Johnson for Retailing Spiritous Liquor Without License.

We present William Sorrows for Retailing Spiritous Liquor Without License.

We present Charles Stewart for Retailing Spiritous Liquor ~~Without License~~ at Capt Brookses Muster Ground without License.

We present Thomas Moody for Retailing Spiritous Liquor Without License.

We present Captin W. Muntford Stokes, James Thompson, Seymour Lee, & Joseph Waters for not Inforcing the patrole Law in their Several Districts.

We present as a Greviance that the Time Appointed for holding the Superior & Inferior Courts for this County is two Short.

We present as a Greviance that a five Alley is Errected on the publick   [146] Square to the Great Interuption of publick Business.

We, the Grand Jury, Return our thanks to his honor the Judge for his Judicious Charge Delivered to us at the Commencement of this Term and also for his unremitted Attention in the faithfull Discharge of his Office.

John Davenport, F. man		Joseph Hubbard
Thomas Gilmore	Isaac Collier	John Luckie
James Freeman	Charles Hay	John George
James Bradley	Noel Thornton	William Jennings
Charles Allen	Middleton Brooks	George Doggett
William Callihan	Reuben Glaze	James Rutledge
	Robert Haynes	

For the purpose of Carrying the Constitution as Revised, amended, & Complied, on the 30th day of May 1798, into as Speedy & Complete Effect as possible under the Existing Circumstances, The Judges and Mr Solicitor Van Allen have and do hereby Establish for the Government of practitioners & Others in the Superior Courts of the Said State, the following as Additional Rules, that is to say, The mode of Carrying Errors in Inferior Judicatories Shall be as follows.

The person Intitled to a Writ of Certiorari to Remove procedings from the Courts Below Shall within four days After Trial in the Said

Courts Serve the Opesite party, or his Council, With a notice in Writing   [147] Stating the grounds on Which he means to say that he will, on the first day or as Soon thereafter as Council Can be heard, Move the Presiding Judges of the Next Superior Court of Said County for a Writ of Certiorari to remove the said proceeding.

On hearing the parties, if the Judge Should grant the writ, The proceedings Shall Be Brought up Instanter, entered on the docket, & be Tried at the Next Succeeding

129

Term of the Superior Court. the party Obtaining the Writ of Certiorari Shall, previous to docketing the proceedings for a new trial, enter into Special Bail & pay Cost, as has been usual heretofore in Cases of Appeal. in Such Cases as have been determined in the Inferior Courts & Appeals granted thereon Since the Adoption of the present Constitution & prior to the promulgation of the Additional rules, the party so Circumstanced applying for a new Trial Shall give Notice in Writing to the Adverse party, or his Council, Stating the grounds on Which he means to move, on or before the first day of the Next Superior Court of the County Where the Appeal Shall have been Entered.

In Cases When Applications Shall Be made for a New Trial after one had at Common Law in the Superior Courts, the party dissatisfied, After Due Notice in Writing to the Oppesite party, or his Council, Stating the Case in Which the Application is founded, may Obtain a rule to Shew Cause, on or before the last day of the Term in Which the Trial was had, why a New Trial Should Not be Granted, & if Such rule is made Absolute, the party Applying Shall give Security & pay Cost, as in Cases of Appeal heretofore used, thereupon the Same Shall be Docketed & Stand for Trial at the Next Term.

That whenever a party in a Cause Shall make his [blot] in Issuing out a Subpona to Compell the Attendance of a Witness

Residing Out of the County Where the Cause may be depending in   [148] preferance to a Commission, the party Abide by Such Election.

That in All Cases of Special Bail or Where Security hath been given heretofore in Cases of Appeal, the plaintiff Shall, in order to make the Bail answerable Equally with the principal, resort to his Ca Sa Against principal & Sa fa Against Bail, According to rules laid Down in the Books.

That Writs of Sa fa Issued to revive Judgments Shall be made returnable to the Next Superior Court of the County Where the Defendant or Defendants, reside, the party Suing Out Such Writ Shall preserve the Exemplification of the record to be Sent to the Clerk of the County Where the Writ is made returnable, on Which Such Judgment or Judgments may be revived.

That When Presentments Shall be made by a Grand Jury of an Indictable Nature, it Shall be the Duty of the State's Attorney & Solicitor to frame Bills of Indictments upon the presentments & the Persons presented Shall Answer to the Bill So framed Without prefering the Said Bill to the Same or Second Grand Jury.

Extracts from the Minutes of the Commission of the Judges.

Jn° L. Dixon, Clk

14th July 1798

Jessee Sanders & }
Henry Hampton }
    vs   }
Ferdinand Phinizy }

Mr Griffin Please to Take Notice the next Term a rule will be applied for in behalf of the Plaintiffs in the Above Case to Shew Cause Why a New Trial may Not be Granted on the following grounds, first because a Verdict was found Contrary to law. Secondly Against [blank]

Georgia   }   [149]
Oglethorpe County } Superior Court October 2nd 1798

Jane Musgrove & Others }
Executrix & Executors of }
the last Will & Testament }
of Harrison Musgrove, Dec^d }
        vs   } Petition for Foreclosure
Benjⁿ Allin & Adnisam Allin }

Upon the Petition of Jane Musgrove, Thomas Gordon, Glen Owen, & John T. Sankey, Executrix & Executors of the last Will & Testament of Harrason Musgrove, Dec^d, Praying the foreclosure of the Equity of redemption in & to a Certain Tract of land, Containing by Estimation One Thousand Acres, lying in the Now County of Oglethorpe, formerly Wilkes, Buting & Bounding North West by Vacant, Surveyed, & William Few's land, North East by Felden's, Nathan Nall's land, & Vacant land, & South Westardly by ~~Vacant~~ Surveyed land, Mortgaged by Ben^j Allin & Adnesam Allin to the State of Georgia, Which Said Mortgage has been Assigned Over from the State of Georgia to the Said Executrix & Executors, & on Motion of John Mathews, Attorney for the Petitioners, it is Ordered the principal, Interest, & Cost upon Said Mortgage be paid in Court, Within Twelve months from this date, & unless the Same be So paid, the Equity of redemption Will from thence fourth be forever barred & foreclosed, & Other Proceedings Take place in pursuance of the Act of the General Assembly in Such Case made & provided.

131

The State   }
   vs   }
Robert Lumpkin }
& David Allin   }

Robt Lumpkin being Sollemly Caled & did Not Appear & David Allin being Also Caled to produce the Body of Robt Lumpkin, he failing to produce him, on Motion of the Solicitor Genl, Ordered that the recognizance be estraited [blot]

John S[blot]   }   [150]
   vs   }
Giles Thompkins   }

Humphrey Thompkins Came forward & Entered himself Special Bail for Giles Thompkins, that is to Say, for the Sum mentioned in the Bail Bond, if the Defendant fails to pay the Sum mentioned in the Bail Bond, I will do it for him or Deliver him in discharge. Taken & Acknowledged in Open Court this Second Day of October 1798.

Test. Jn° Lumpkin, Clk   Giles Thompkins
                                     Hum. Thompkins

Ordered, that all Grand Jurors Who have made Default at the present Term be fined Twenty dollars Each, unless they do Shew good & Sufficient Cause of Excuse Within Thirty days from the first day of the Present Term upon Oath & file the Same in the Clerk's Office.

Also Ordered, that all Pettit Jurors Who have made default at the present Term be fined Ten Dollars Each, unless they do Shew the like Cause of Excuse Within the Same time & file the Same in the Clerk's Office in like manner.

Examined.   D. B. Mitchell

Grand Jurors Drawn for Next Term

1. John Stewart, Genl 16. William Daniel
2. Fleming Jorden   17. Abram Hill
3. Thomas Moody   18. Joseph Lumpkin, Senr
4. William Green   19. Reubin Jordin
5. William Smith   20. Bennett Hubbard
6. William M. Bledsoe   21. Burwell Pope

7. William Embry
8. Jnᵒ Garrott
9. Amos Ponder
10. Samuel Strong
11. James Thompson
12. Benʲ Fry
13. Micajah Clark
14. Theophilus Allison
15. [blot] Wagnan

22. Herrod Thornton, Senʳ
23. Thomas Meareweather
24. Nicholas Johnson
25. Ferdinand Phinizy
26. Thomas Hughs
27. Benʲ Wilks
28. Joseph Wise
29. Robert Beavers
30. Phillip Wray
31. Charles Smith
32. Jnᵒ C. Evans

Pettit Jurors Drawn for Next Term [151]

1. Thomas Loyd, Senʳ
2. George Hodge
3. Robert Armstrong
4. John Taylor
5. David Lindsey
6. Sherwood Wilkerson
7. Osnon Whatley
8. Jeremiah Elsbury
9. Archebel Tanner
10. William Peters
11. John Johnson
12. Burwell House
13. Geᵒ Bailey
14. John Bowles
15. Stewart Cowin
16. John Young
17. Robert Young
18. Goldson Copland
19. Henry Bradshaw
20. Archebel Ramsey
21. William Ba[smear]
22. William Hardman
23. William Camwell
24. George Smith
25. William McElroy
26. Arther Foster

31. William Richards
32. James Hunt
33. James Devenport
34. William Norris
35. Joseph Elsbury
36. William Thompson
37. Abel Mcintosh
38. Chatten Scoggin
39. David Patrick
40. Isaac Penington
41. William Stephens
42. Jacob Hinton
43. Plesant Compton
44. Josiah Whitlock
45. Jessee Clay
46. John Thomas
47. Miles Hill
48. Benʲ Elsbury
49. John Fluker
50. Michael Moore
51. Jessee Lee
52. Phelps Haynes
53. Jacob Hodge
54. James Spurlock
55. John Dawson
56. John Wray

133

27. Huriah Gilmer	57. William Biars
28. Henry Tyler	58. William Richerson
29. Michael Woodall	59. William Edwards
30. Hrad Thornton	60. John Fullerlove

Jessee Sanders & }
Henry Hampton }
    vs   } Covenant
Ferdinand Phinizy }

[152]

We, the Plaintiffs in the Above Case, being Dissatisfied With the Judgment of the Jury, do Enter an Appeal to a Special Jury, & Henry Hill & E. Booker Jinkins Came forward and Entered themselves Security for the Eventual Condemnation Money, or to Surrender the plaintiffs in Discharge, or we will do it for them. Taken And Acknowledged this 2nd day of October 1798.

Test. Jno Lumpkin, Clk

                         Jessee Sanders
                         Henry Hampton
                         Henry Hill
                         Ed^m B. Jinkins

At a Superior Court Begun & Held in & for The County of Oglethorpe on The 28th day of March 1799. Present, His Honor Judge Carnes.

John Christian }
    vs   }
John Moore   }

Pettit Jury N° 1 Sworn

1. Thomas Loyd	5. G. Smith	9. Joseph Elsbury
2. Archebel Tanner	6. William Hardman	10. Isaac Penington
3. William Peters	7. Dread Thornton	11. Jacob Hinton
4. Stewart Cowin	8. James Devenport	12. James Hunt

We, the Jury, find for the Plaintiff One hundred and forty Dollars, With Cost.

                         James Davenport, F. man

Johnson Strong   }
Samuel E[smear]   }
     vs   } Debt
William M. Stoakes }

Jury Sworn N° 2

1. Jessee Clay	5. William Biars	9. Peter Smith
2. Miles Hill	6. William Edwards	10. Joseph Embry
3. Benj^m Elsbury	7. James Hay	11. Jacob Lorance
4. Jessee Lee	8. John Hawkins	12. Nathaniel Bradford

We, the Jury, Agree Each party Shall pay his Own Cost.

James Hay, F. man

Grand Jurors Sworn

1. Jn° Stewart, F. man	9. William Daniel	16. Joel Barnett
2. William Smith	10. Burwell Pope	17. James Thomas
3. Wm M. Bledsoe	11. Nicholas Johnson	18. Thomas Gilmer
4. William Embry	12. Benjamin Wilks	19. Leonard Young
5. Amus Ponder	13. Ferdinand Phinizy	20. Joshua Martin
6. Benjamin Frys	14. Thomas Moody	21. Abram Hill
7. Micajah Clark	15. John Banks	22. Charles Smith

Charles Burk }
    vs   } Ejectment
Stephen Hurd }

Upon Suggestion that the land in dispute between the parties formerly lying in Oglethorpe & That by the Act of the last Legislature That part of Oglethorpe in Which the land lay was Taken of from Oglethorpe & aded to Greene. It is Ordered, that All the Papers relative to the above Suit be Carefully Sealed up by the Clerk of this Court & Transmited to the Clerk of the Superior Court of Greene County & That the Said Clerk Docket the Said Cause in the Superior Court of Said County upon the Trial Dockquitt.

Benjamin Baldwin }
& Douglas Watson, Exo^{rs} }
of Joshua Thornton, Dec^d }
      vs   } Debt
Nathaniel Durkie & }
Cudberth Coleman }

Jury N° 1, Except Josiah Jordon in the place of William Hardman.

We find for the Plaintiffs Two hundred & Twelve Dollars & forty Cents Against Coleman, Whom the Writ was Serv^d.

John Davenport, F. man

Thos P. Carnes

The Honorable Court Then Adjourned till Tomorrow 9 O'Clock.

The Honorable Court Met Agreeable to Adjournment Friday 29th March 1799. Present, His Honor Thos P. Carnes.

James Edwards, Ass^{ee} }
of Hezekiah Solomon }
      vs   } Debt
Spencer Reynolds }

Jury N° 1

1. Thomas Loyd	5. George Smith	9. William Green
2. Archer Tanner	6. Isaac Penington	10. William Hardman
3. William Peters	7. Jacob Hinton	11. Abel Penington
4. Stewart Cowin	8. John Taylor	12. John Hail

We, The Jury, find for the Plaintiff One hundred and Seventeen Dollars, With Cost.

Ge^o Smith, F. man

Thomas Flint}
      vs   } Case
Peter Hawk }

Jury N° 1 as Above.

We find for the plaintiff forty Dollars, With Cost.

Ge° Smith, F. man

Shadrick Kennebrew   }   [155]
      vs   } Debt
Jn° Moore & Jn° Lumpkin }

Jury Sworn N° 2

1. Jessee Clay   5. William Biars   9. Jacob Lorance
2. Miles Hill   6. William Edwards   10. Nathaniel Bradford
3. Benjamin Elsbury   7. John Hawkins   11. Peter Hoof
4. Jessee Lee   8. Joseph Embry   12. John Bradley

We find for the Plaintiff Two hundred & fifty Dollars, With Interest from the first day of December 1797 & Cost.

Jessee Clay, F. man

John Hines   }
    vs   } Case
Josiah Hatcher }

Jury N° 1 Sworn

1. Thomas Loyd   5. George Smith   9. William Green
2. Archer Tanner   6. Isaac Penington   10. William Hardman
3. William Peters   7. Jacob Hinton   11. Abel Penington
4. Stewart Cowin   8. John Taylor   12. John Hail

We, the Jury, find for the Plaintiff Eighty Six Dollars, With Cost.

Ge° Smith, F. man

James Bown   }
    vs   } Case
James Stovall }

Jury N° 2 as last.

We, the Jury, find for the plaintiff Eighty One Dollars & Ninety Seven Cents.

Jessee Clay, F. man

John Michael   }
Surviving Cop^r   }
of Michael & Sims }
        vs   } Case
Alaxander Jordon }

Jury N° 1 As Above.

We, the Jury, find for the plaintiff forty Eight Dollars, With Cost.

Ge° Smith, F. man

John Parks   }   [156]
    vs   } Pett in Equity
Josiah Jordon }

It Appearing that the Answer had Not been filed Within time.

Ordered by the Court, on Motion of Mr Walker, Sol^r for the Defendant, that the Said Answer be filed nunc pro tunc & the Cause be Set Down for Trial Tomorrow morning on the Bill & Answer.

John Griffin, Adm^r   }
of Harwood Goodwin, Dec^d }
        vs   }
Thomas Loyd & Ann Loyd   }
Adm^{rs} of B. Bridgman, Dec^d }

Jury N° 2

We do find for the Plaintiffs Two hundred & fifty five Dollars Twenty Cents, With Cost & Interest.

Jessee Clay, F. man

138

Charles McDonald }
    vs   } Debt
Joseph Wilson   }

Judgment Confessed for the Sum of Thirty One dollars & Seventy Eight Cents, With Interest from the Twenty fourth Day of June 1790 untill paid, & Cost of Suit, With Stay of Levey four months.

Test. Jn° Lumpkin, Clk   Joseph Wilson
                                29th March 1799

Hugh Freman, Senr }
    vs   }
Alaxander Gordon }
& Samuel Gardner }

Upon Motion of Mr Griffin, Attorney for the plaintiff, it is Ordered that a rule of Survey be Granted, Directed to the County Surveyor, or his Deputy, Authorising & requiring him or Either of them to Lay of & Admeasure the land in dispute, lawfully Distinguishing the Marks & Bounds of the Same & Also

Wheather the Land in dispute & how much is Contained Within the   [157] Tract or Survey of land Claimed by the plaintiff both the parties, & Also Intitled to take on the ground the Day of Survey one Assistant Surveyor Each of their Own Choice, & the Plaintiff is hereby Directed to give Five Days Notice Previous to his having the Said Survey made.

Samuel Williamson }
    vs   } Pets & pro
John Gresham   }

Jury N° 2 Sworn

1. James Brooks	5. William Biars	9. Dread Thornton
2. Joshua Glass	6. William Edwards	10. Jacob Lorance
3. Benjamin Elsbury	7. John Hawkins	11. Peter Hoof
4. Jessee Lee	8. James Hitchcock	12. John Bradley

We do find for the Plaintiff forty Two Dollars Eighty Six Cents, With Interest & Cost of Suit.

James Bradley, F. man

Jnᵒ Wilson   }
     vs   }
Presley Thornton }

Appeal Special Jury

Jury Sworn

1. John Stewart	5. Amus Ponder	9. Burwell Pope
2. William Smith	6. Micajah Clark	10. Nicholas Johnson
3. William M. Bledsoe	7. Theᵒ Allison	11. Benjamin Wilks
4. William Embry	8. William Daniel	12. Thomas Moody

We, the Jury, find for the Appellant Two Dollars 35¼ Cents, With Cost.

John Stewart, F. man

William Hughs }   [158]
     vs   } Caveat from Register's Office
Timothy Harris }

On Motion, it is Ordered that Letters of Administration be Granted to William Hughs of All & Singular the rights & Credits of Allen Johnson, Deceased, in persuance to his Application made to the Register of Probates for the County of Oglethorpe, & that the Order in favour of Henry Hill made at the last Term by Consent be recinded, he Not having Complied With the Conditions of Said Consent.

James Edwards }
     vs   }
Spencer Reynolds }

Spencer Reynolds Came forward With William Strother, Security, for The Stay of Execution Sixty Days, the Security Binds himself to pay the Eventual

Condemnation money if the Defendant fails to do it. Taken & Acknowledged before me the 30th day of March 1799.

Test. Jnº Lumpkin, Clk   Spencer Reynolds
                                           William Strother

Exd   Thº P. Carnes

The Court then Adjourned till 9 O'Clock Tomorrow Morning.

The Honorable Court Met Agreeable to Adjournment. Present, His Honor Thos P. Carnes.

John Ralston, Assignee }   [159]
of Nathaniel Durkee   }
            vs   }
John Stewart   }

In this Case, the Clerk reported that there Never Was a Writ of this Kind in his Office, that it Was Dockquited by the Consent of the parties, & now at this day the Plaintiff and his Council failing to Appear & furnish a process on Which a Verdict Could pass, it is Considered this Action is improperly on the Docket & is of as if the Same had never appeared.

Francis Gordon }
        vs   } Illegality
John Moore   }

Execution Set aside on the Grounds of Its Issuing from a Court Other than the One Where the Judgment Was Obtained, & in this as All Other cases Similar Where the Appeal may have been With drawn or Dismised, the Clerk of this Court Will return the papers to the Court below.

John Griffin &   }
Thomas Goodwin, Aplts {
        vs   } Appeal Trover
James Brookes, Respt   }

141

1. John Stewart	5. Amus Ponder	9. Burwell Pope
2. William Smith	6. Micajah Clark	10. Nicholas Johnson
3. Wm M. Bledsoe	7. The^o Allison	11. Ben^j Wilks
4. William Embry	8. William Daniel	12. Joel Barnett

We find for the Appellant the Negro & her Increase or four hundred Dollars.

John Stewart, F. man

David Creswell, Ap^{lt} }   [160]
   vs   }
Jared Banks   }

In This Case, it is Ordered that With the Consent of parties John Gresham be made a party to the Above.

John Gresham &   }
David Creswell, Apl^{ts} }
   vs   } Appeal
Jared Banks   }

1. John Stewart	5. Amus Ponder	9. Burwell Pope
2. William Smith	6. Micajah Clark	10. Nic. Johnson
3. Wm M. Bledsoe	7. The^o Allison	11. Ben^j Wilks
4. Wm Embry	8. William Daniel	12. Joel Barnett

We find for the Respondent four hundred & Twenty Six dollars Eughteen Cents, With Interest & Cost.

John Stewart, F. man

Nathaniel Moss & }
Samuel Moss, Apl^{ts} }
    vs   } Appeal
Alaxander Moss   }

1. John Stewart   5. Amus Ponder   9. Nicholas Johnson
2. William Smith   6. Micajah Clark   10. Ben^j Wilks
3. Wm M. Bledsoe   7. The^o Allison   11. Joel Barnett
4. Wm Embry   8. William Daniel   12. James Thomas

We, the Jury, find for the respondant.

John Stewart, F. man

John Parks   }
    vs   }   Bill in Equity
Josiah Jordon }

Continued.

Ex^d Thos P. Carnes

The Court Then Adjourned untill Monday Morning 9 O'Clock.   [161]

The Honorable Court Met on Monday the 1st of April 1799. Present, his honor Thos P. Carnes.

The Following Persons Were Drawn to Serve as Grand & Pettit Jurors. (To Witt)

Grand Jurors

1. Micajah McGhee   16. Henry Hill
2. Joshua Martin   17. John Grimes
3. William Harvie   18. Hugh Ector
4. Joseph Morton   19. James Northington
5. John Griffin   20. Alaxander Commings
6. Jeffery Early   21. William Graves
7. George Phillips   22. William Walker
8. James Smith   23. Edward Powell
9. Richardson Hamner   24. Reubin Embry
10. James Luckie   25. John Smith
11. Nicholas Hawkins   26. Isham Berry
12. John Collier   27. James Hay
13. John Moore   28. Pitman Lumpkin

14. William Berry
15. William George, Jun[r]

29. Nathaniel Moss
30. John H. Marks

Pettit Jurors

1. Henry Boland
2. Jessee Embry
3. John Eachols
4. John Smith
5. Josiah Goolsbey
6. Isaac Williams
7. James McGhee
8. William Alaxander
9. James Stampts
10. Samuel Gordon
11. Isham Davis
12. Robert Simpson
13. Joseph Lumpkin, Jun[r]
14. David Herring
15. Anthony Noleman
16. William Briant
17. John Little
18. William Goolsbey
19. Henry Hartsfield
20. Hezekiah Luckie
21. Joseph Wilson
22. James Sanders, Jun[r]
23. Sam[l] Harris
24. James East
25. Luke Johnson
26. John Legett
27. Thomas Britton
28. Jeremiah Boggus
29. David Herring, J[r]
30. John Martin
31. Thomas Brooks

32. Thomas Stephens, J[r]
33. Sam[l] Penington
34. Gilbert Keen
35. Joseph Waters
36. William Staton
37. Harmon Holt
38. James Brooks
39. Dunston Banks
40. John Northan
41. Arther Crofford
42. Robert Calquit
43. Edmond Griffin
44. Levee Campill
45. Jeames Kidd
46. Joshua Stephens
47. John Roussaux
48. Charles Stewart
49. William Cowin
50. John Hartsfield
51. Nat Bradford
52. James Sims
53. William Hartsfield
54. James Kadenhead
55. John Belemy
56. William Shields
57. John Britton
58. John Jackson
59. William Jones
60. Hawkins Bullock
61. Sam[l] McLean
62. George Cross

Ordered that a Viniri facias Issue in the usual form.   [163]

Thomas Gilmer & }
Micajah McGhee }
        vs   }
William Bailey   }

In This Case, it Being Stated to the Court that William Bailey, Esquire, Sheriff of the County, had by Virtue of an Execution Sold & Conveyed to the Plaintiffs a Tract of land, the property of Robert Lumpkin, & in the possession of the Said Robert Lumpkin, & that the Same Still Continues in the Possession of the Said Lumpkin, on Motion it is Ordered, that the Sheriff do Shew Cause on the first day of the Next Term Why he hath Not Delivered possession of the property Aforesaid to the plaintiffs.

Presentments of the Grand Jury

We Present James Pye for Retailing Liquors Without Licence.

We Present Levie Jinnings for Retailing Liquors Without Licence.

We Present the Surveyors of the road from the Goosepond Creek to long Creek, it Being the Augusta road.

We present as a greavance that the Defaulting Jurors Are Not fined.

We Present Thomas Duke, J[r] for retailing Liquors Without Licence.

We Present Job Wooten for Retailing Liquors Without Licence.   [164]

We Present as a Greavance that the Honorable the Inferior Court do Not take Bond & Security of All those Whom they have Granted Licence to keep Publick houses Agreeable to Law.

We Present Mathew Gage for Retailing Liquors Without Licence.

We return his honor the Judge our thanks for his Juditious Charge to the Grand Jury & his Strict Attention to the Duties of his Important Office.

John Stewart, F. man	Nicholas Johnson
Joel Barnett	Benjamin Wilks

145

William Smith	Thomas Moody
William M. Bledsoe	James Thomas
William Embry	Thomas Gilmer
Amus Ponder	Abram Hill
Micajah Clark	Charles Smith
Theo Allison	Theo Hill
William Daniel	

The Presentments of the Grand Jury being under Consideration, it is [165] Ordered that the first, Second, fifth, Sixth, & Seventh be provided over by the Solicitor Genl & that a Copy of the third & fourth presentments be made Out, Certified, & Transmitted by the Clerk of this Court to the Honorable the Inferior Court on the first Day of the Next Term of the Said Inferior Court.

James Brooks }
   An Sev } Trover
Adm\ rs of Goodwin }

On Motion of M\ r Walters, Council four the Defendant, James Brooks, Ordered that the Plaintiffs, Thomas Goodwin & John Griffin, Adm\ rs, Shew Cause on the first day of the Next Term or as Soon thereafter as Council Can be heard, Why a New Trial Should Not be Granted in the Above Case, & it is further Ordered that a Copy of this rule, together With the grounds of the Application, be Served on Either of the plaintiffs, or their Attorney, Twenty Days before the Siting of this Next Court.

Examined.   Tho\ s P. Carnes
                             1\ st April 1799

The Court then Adjourned till Court in Course.

Index

___
John, 47
Thomas, 63
Acre
John, 77, 86, 88, 92
Adams
Godfrey, 66
Addams
Godfrey, 92
Adkinson
Nathan, 96
Thomas, 96
Alaxander
Edmond, 47, 49
Edmonds, 53
Joseph, 56, 72
Sarah, 72, 74, 78
Smith, 55, 72
William, 144
Aldridge
Abner, 88
Alexander
Edmd., 38, 40
Allen, 59
Charles, 117, 120, 123, 124, 125, 129
Wm., 4
Allin
Adnesam, 131
Adnisam, 131
Benj., 131
David, 132
P., 107
Peter V., 41
William, 43
Allison

Theo, 140, 142, 143, 146
Theophilus, 80, 133
Theops., 80
Anderson
John, 19, 22
John N., 34
Andrews
Alax, 117
John, 42, 54, 55
Nathan, 23
Anthony
Jno., 22
John, 19
Armstrong
Jas., 34
Robert, 133
Arnold
John, 22
John, Sr., 19
Thomas, 19
Thos., 22
Zachh., 34
Arther
William, 107
Asbury
Richard, 118
Askew
Joshua, 81, 103, 114
Averhart
Jacob, 64
B___
James, 102
Ba___
William, 133
Bagley
Joshua, 52

Bailey, 76
  Geo., 133
  John, 33, 77
  Richard, 9, 30, 33, 88
  Richd., 39
  William, 145
Baily
  Richard, 54
Baird
  Jonathan, 77
Balcher
  Benjamin, 77
Baldwin
  Ann, 109
  Benj., 103
  Benjamin, 96, 116, 136
  David, 109
  Ephraim, 109
  Owen, 109
  William, 109
Banks
  Dunstan, 23
  Dunston, 121, 122, 126, 144
  Gerald, 105
  Gerard, 119
  Jared, 142
  John, 77, 78, 87, 121, 126, 135
Barber, 113
  Geo., 31, 45
Barnard
  Zadock, 43
Barnet
  Joel, 55, 56
  Zadock, 48, 49, 53
Barnett
  Benj., 117
  Claburn, 117
  Joel, 42, 43, 58, 60, 135, 142, 143, 145
  Zaddock, 29

Battlesby
  William, 23
Baugh
  Joseph, 62
Baugus
  Jeremiah, 62
Bayley
  Richard, 46
Beasley
  John, 63
  Robert, 97, 117
  William, 108
  Wm., 117, 120, 121
Beasly
  William, 116
Beavers
  Joseph, 96, 98
  Robert, 5, 77, 87, 99, 133
  Robt., 4
Beckers
  Robert, 63
Belcher
  Obediah, 47, 49, 54, 63
Belemy
  John, 144
Bell
  A., 94
  Andrew, 4, 5, 16, 57, 62, 63, 87, 94, 99
  Henry, 88, 90, 93, 94
  Walter, 4
Bellamy
  John, 23, 24
  Richard, 23
Bennett
  Charity, 91
Berry
  Isham, 143
  William, 62, 63, 144
Biars

William, 134, 135, 137, 139
Wm., 34
Biddle
  Abner, 42
  Absolum, 42
Biers
  William, 7, 20
  Wm., 4
Bird
  Phillimon, 77
Black
  Lemuel, 48, 72, 74, 105, 115
  Thomas, 15, 31, 42, 77
Blake
  Benja., 33, 37
  Benjamin, 62
Blakley
  John, 77
Blanton
  John, 29, 34, 64, 73, 124
Bledsoe
  Peachey, 23
  Peachy, 22
  Pechee, 104, 111
  Pechy, 111
  Peechy, 37
  William, 42, 43, 58, 60, 73, 96,
    100
  William M., 132, 140, 146
  Wm., 58, 113
  Wm. M., 135, 142, 143
Bogges
  Jeremiah, 34, 39
Boggus
  Jarh., 72
  Jeremiah, 38, 64, 66, 70, 79, 80,
    144
Bohanan
  Edmd., 22
  K., 62

Bohannan
  Edmd., 38, 39
  Edwd., 34
Bohannon
  Jas., 120
  William, 48
Bohanon
  Jas., 117
Boland
  Frederick, 51
  Henry, 144
  Richard, 23, 24, 43, 47, 50, 54
Boles
  John, 52
Boling
  Saml., 120
  Samuel, 128
Bolling
  Saml., 117
Borum
  George, 121, 126
Bouchanan
  Edmond, 19
Bowen
  Jos., 4
Bowland
  Richard, 57
Bowles
  John, 133
Bowls
  William, 96
Bown
  James, 137
Bradford
  N., 104
  Nat, 144
  Nathaniel, 78, 86, 104, 135, 137
  Nathl., 104
Bradley

James, 117, 120, 124, 125, 129, 140
Jas., 123, 124
John, 137, 139
Bradshaw
Henry, 133
Brag
Dorias, 43
Bragg
Dasher, 103
Branham
Spencer, 69
Brewer
Burwell, 57, 92
Edward, 64
Elisha, 72
Patrick, 92
Briant
William, 144
Bridges
Baines, 32
Benjamin, 52
Berry, 32
David, 19, 32
Jesse, 32
John, 32, 77
Jonathan, 34
Jones, 32
Merett, 32
Nancy, 32
Nathaniel, 32
Nathl., 88
Bridgman
B., 138
Britton
John, 62, 144
Thomas, 144
Brook
James, 74
Brookes

James, 141
John, 89
Brooks, 128
James, 46, 74, 88, 139, 144, 146
Middleton, 19, 22, 78, 86, 89, 92, 117, 120, 123, 124, 125, 129
Thomas, 121, 126, 144
Broton
James, 88
Brown, 96
Alexander, 23, 24
Alexr., 29
Burwell, 96
Elisha, 48, 74
Elizabeth, 96
Thomas, 96, 105, 111
William, 43, 45
Bruer
Burwell, 39
Bryant
William, 23
Buckner
John, 64, 87
Bullock
Hawkins, 62, 144
Nathaniel, 108, 111, 125
Burford
Daniel, 24
Soloman, 43
Solomon, 47, 50, 53
Burk
Charles, 22, 32, 56, 62, 63, 76, 105, 111, 114, 135
Charles, Jr., 97, 111
Charles, Sr., 111
Chas., 18
Burnes
John W., 44, 70
Burton
Jacob, 19, 22

Bustin
  Benjamin, 94, 101
Calaway
  Job, 105, 110
Call
  Richard, 127, 128
Callahan
  John, 43
  Wm., 117, 120
Callaway
  Job, 96
Callier, 55
  James, 44
  John, 34, 40, 41, 42, 44, 53, 56
Callihan
  William, 125, 129
  Wm., 123, 124
Calquit
  Robert, 144
Campbell
  Charles, 15
  Charles, Sr., 15
Campell
  Robert, 92
Campill
  Levee, 144
Camwell
  William, 133
Canterbury
  Joseph, 80
Caragan
  Wm., 117
Cardin
  Wm., 120
Cargile
  Charles, 62, 63
  Jno., 40
  John, 37, 38, 96, 100, 113
Cargill
  John, 12, 33

Carnes, 65, 104, 109, 134
  Tho. P., 141
  Thomas P., 100, 116
  Thos. P., 103, 116, 136, 141, 143,
    146
  Ths. P., 119
Carr
  Josiah, 96, 105, 110
  Thomas, 128
Carrington
  Timothy, 15
Carter, 24
  Blake, 96
  Cornelius, 23
  Isa, 24
  Jacob, 18, 22, 47, 49
  Thomas, 38, 39, 93, 99
Cartright
  Peter, 49, 63
Cartwright, 89
  Peter, 28
Carvenah, 15
Casey
  William, 63
Catching
  Joseph, 37
Catchings
  Joseph, 22, 23
Cauldwell
  Hy., 86
Cavenah
  Charles, 9, 12, 13, 14, 19
Chandler
  Parks, 34, 38, 39
Christian
  Elijah, 100
  John, 113, 134
Claghorn
  John, 14, 17
Clark

Johnson, 63
Micajah, 62, 63, 133, 135, 140,
142, 143, 146
Clarke
Elijah, 27
Johnson, 4, 7
Micajah, 19, 22, 23
Clay, 81
Jesse, 4, 5, 11, 13, 16
Jessee, 79, 81, 105, 133, 135, 137,
138
Royal, 66, 81
Clendennal
Mat, 63
Coats
William, 86
Cochran
Mary, 31
Coldwell
William, 117
Cole
John, 34, 38, 39, 78
Josiah, 4, 5, 8, 11, 12, 14, 22, 23,
37
Coleman
Cudberth, 103, 116, 136
Jesse, 4
Colley
Salley, 32
Zacharias, 32
Collier
Cudberth, 105
Isaac, 4, 5, 16, 62, 63, 117, 120,
123, 124, 125, 129
John, 4, 5, 16, 143
Vines, 4
Colloy
James, 126
Colquit
Saml., 58, 60

Colquitt
Samuel, 43
Combs
John, 23, 29
Commings
Alaxander, 143
Compton
Plesant, 133
Plesent, 55
Cooper
Thomas, 25, 26
Copland
Goldson, 133
Richard, 27
Richd., 38
Cowen
George, 38, 40
Cowin
George, 77
James, 43, 47, 50, 53
Stewart, 133, 134, 136, 137
William, 144
Cragg
James, 49
Crane
Thomas, 19, 22
Creswell
D., 119, 120
David, 105, 142
Crews
Ethelord, 77
Crofford
Arther, 144
Croley
John, 77
Cross
Geo., 62, 68, 73
George, 71, 79, 80, 144
Cruchfield
Robert, 77

Cummins
Alex, 128
Cumtton
Plesent, 80
Cunningham
John, 23
Daniel
Charles, 109
Edmond, 42, 68
Edmund, 23
James, 33, 96
James, Jr., 96, 100, 113
Thomas, 26
William, 132, 135, 140, 142, 143, 146
Darrity
Charles, 62
Davenport
James, 18, 22, 134
John, 120, 121, 122, 126, 127, 129, 136
Davis
Isam, 126
Isham, 4, 13, 14, 18, 20, 144
Dawson
John, 133
Demontrony
Duham, 16, 25
Denn
John, 108
Devenport
James, 64, 78, 87, 99, 133, 134
James, Jr., 64
James, Sr., 64
Jas., 88
John, 62, 117
Dicken
Jereh., 22
Jeremh., 19
Jeremiah, 11

Dickens
Jeremiah, 12
Dickins
Jeremiah, 43
Dimond
John, 8, 18, 115, 122
Dixon
Jno. L., 131
Doe, 96
John, 29, 53, 109
Dogget
George, 124
Millery, 124
Doggett
George, 120, 129
Doggit
Geo., 63
George, 117
Thomas, 87
William, 105
Downs
Henry, 33
Henry D., 53, 115, 118
Duke
Thomas, 18, 22, 27, 62
Thomas, Jr., 145
William, 77
Dun
John, 58
Joseph, 96
Thomas, 43, 60
Duncan
Wm., 54, 57
Dunn
John, 42, 43, 60, 116
Thomas, 66, 67, 96
Dunstan
John, 34
Durham
Saml., 29

Samuel, 23, 24
Durkee
 Nathaniel, 103, 141
Durkie
 Nathaniel, 26, 116, 136
 Nathl., 25
E___
 Samuel, 135
Eachols
 John, 144
Eakols
 John, 90
Ealey
 Jessee, 105, 110
 William, 48, 62
 Wm., 96
Ealy
 Jessee, 96
 William, 49, 105, 111
Earley, 123
 Jeffrey, 30, 37, 38, 120, 123
Early
 Jeffery, 143
 Jeffrey, 4, 5, 13, 16, 23, 25, 26,
  27, 29, 34, 38, 40, 47, 51, 53,
  65, 67, 69, 74, 80, 87, 107, 114
 Peter, 41
Easley
 R., 120
 Roderick, 119
Easly
 Jeffrey, 77
Eason
 Abram, 87
East
 James, 10, 14, 25, 26, 43, 144
 James, Jr., 15
 Wm., 45
Easter
 Abraham, 18, 22

William, 43, 54
Easton
 William, 57
Echols
 John, 17
Eckols
 Joseph, 10
Ector
 Hugh, 18, 22, 38, 40, 62, 63, 143
Edmondson
 Humpy., 4, 5
Edmonson
 Charles, 62
 Humphrey, 16, 38, 51, 68, 77, 93,
  99, 128
 Humpy., 39
 Phil, 96
 Phillip, 34, 66
 Thomas, 43
Edward
 Benjamin, 44
Edwards
 Benj., 77
 Edmond, 43
 James, 101, 136, 140
 John, 18
 Nathan, 19, 22
 William, 75, 107, 114, 121, 134,
  135, 137, 139
Ellerson
 Thos., 44
Elliot
 Geo., 43
 Robert, 77
Ellis
 Radford, 19, 22, 24, 29, 47
 Radford, Jr., 23
Ellison
 Theophilus, 18, 22
Ellott

154

Robert, 88, 89, 92
Ellsberry
  Joseph, 22
Ellsbury
  Joseph, 18
Elsburey
  Jacob, 88
Elsbury
  Benj., 133, 135
  Benjamin, 137, 139
  Jacob, 77, 86, 92, 104, 105, 115,
    116
  Jeremiah, 133
  Joseph, 133, 134
Emberson
  ___, 51
Embrey
  John, 43
  Joseph, 43
Embry
  Jas., 54, 57
  Jessee, 144
  John, 54, 96, 100, 113
  Joseph, 57, 135, 137
  Reubin, 77, 86, 88, 143
  William, 133, 135, 140, 142, 146
  Wm., 142, 143
Espey
  Joseph, 117
Evans
  Jno. C., 133
Everalt
  Jacob, 79
Everart
  Jacob, 80
Everhart
  Jacob, 19, 22, 63
Farer
  Geo., 117
Farrow

George, 120, 128
Farson
  John, 112
Felden, 131
Felton
  Jacob, 23
Fenly
  Joseph, 63
Fenn
  Richard, 108, 116
Fenning
  John, 43
Few
  William, 131
  Wm., 86
Finch
  Burdit, 96
  Charles, 27, 43, 71, 73, 92, 100
Fleming
  John, 60, 67
Fletcher, 20
  Jereh., 22
  Jeremiah, 19
  William, 12, 20
  Wm., 11
Flint
  Tapley, 64, 66, 70, 72
  Taply, 57, 62
  Thomas, 136
Flournoy
  Robert, 105, 111, 114
Floyd
  John, 69, 73
Fluker
  Jno., 52
  John, 77, 87, 99, 108, 111, 125,
    133
Forrester
  Joel, 117
Foster

Arther, 133
John H., 26
Franks
John, 104
Freeman
Hugh, 5, 29
Hugh, Jr., 6
Hugh. Jr., 5
James, 120, 123, 125, 129
Jas., 124
Freman, 48
Holeman, 51
Hugh, 48, 96, 112
Hugh, Sr., 139
James, 100, 113, 117
Noah, 77, 86
William, 78, 88
Fry
Benj., 133
Frys
Benjamin, 135
Fullerlove
John, 134
Gage
Mathew, 145
Galasby
Robert, 7, 20
Robt, 4
Galaspey, 48
Galaspie
Robert, 14
Gallasby
Robert, 16
Gallaspie
Robert, 13
Galloway
Mattw., 19, 22
Gally
Levey, 77
Gammon

Smith, 126
Gardner
Saml., 122
Samuel, 122, 139
Garrett, 17
Henry, 11, 17, 24
John, 4, 5, 16, 22, 23, 37, 51, 62, 63
Garrot
Henry, 53
Garrott
Jno., 133
John, 70, 90, 91, 99
Gaummon
Smith, 43
Geiger
Vallentine, 81
George
Bailey, 105
John, 117, 120, 127, 129
William, Jr., 144
Gholsbey
William, 64
Willliam, 62
Gibbons
Thomas, 28, 29, 30, 31, 32, 47, 48
Gibney
John, 96
Gibson
John, 124
Gilbert
Wm., 117
Gilham
Charles, 128
Gill
Thomas, 96
Gillam
Charles, 120
Gillaspell
James, 68

Gillaspie
  Robt., 71
Gillespie
  Robt., 13
Gillum
  Charles, 117
  Ezekel, 77, 87, 99
Gilmer
  Huriah, 134
  Thomas, 42, 58, 60, 135, 145, 146
  Thos., 58
Gilmor
  Thomas, 117
Gilmore
  John T., 117
  Thomas, 120, 123, 125, 129
  Thomas M., 124, 125, 126
  Thos., 123, 124
Gilner
  Thomas, 43
Ginnings
  Miles, 77
Glass, 109
  Joshua, 109, 139
Glaze
  David, 96
  Reuben, 120, 123, 124, 125, 129
  Reubin, 117
Glazner
  George, 23
Glenn
  James, 63, 68, 70, 72, 79, 80
Goings
  Reuben, 32
Goldsby
  Daniel, 23
  Jno., Jr., 4
  John, 15
  John Kerby, 15
  Nancy, 15

  Peter, 15
  Richd., 4, 5, 16
Golsbey
  William, 96
Good
  Thomas, 105, 106
Goodman
  Jno., 117
Goodwin, 88, 146
  Harwood, 138
  Thomas, 46, 88, 141, 146
Gooldsbey
  Richard, 77
Goolsbey
  Daniel, 77
  Isaak, 77
  Josiah, 144
  Richard, 99
  William, 66, 69, 72, 144
Goolsby
  Daniel, 37
  Isaiah, 126
  James, 30
  John K., 25
  Richard, 87
Gordan
  Alexander, 123
  Francis, 125
Gordon
  Alax, 42
  Alaxander, 58, 102, 139
  Alex, 48
  Alexander, 5, 6, 18, 22, 23, 37
  Alexr., 27, 29
  Fran., 17
  Francis, 8, 16, 26, 141
  Jos., 19, 22
  Samuel, 144
  Thomas, 131
Gosdin

John, 53
Gower
  Abel, 43, 47, 50, 53, 96, 100, 113
Grag
  Joseph, 43
Grands
  Lewis, 63
Graves
  William, 33, 37, 38, 143
Green
  William, 37, 132, 136, 137
Greene
  Benjn., 13
  William, 23
Greenwood
  Beaverly, 79
Greer
  David, 39
  Richard, 117
Gresham
  Harris, 97
  Jno., 72, 119
  John, 42, 72, 105, 139, 142
  John, Sr., 96
  Robert, 39, 96
Greysham
  Edward, 43
Griffin, 34, 76, 77, 88, 112, 131, 139
  Edmond, 144
  J., 108
  John, 6, 46, 70, 73, 77, 88, 138,
    141, 143, 146
Griffith
  John, 30
Grimes
  John, 143
Grisham
  John, 72
Gunnalds
  John, 62, 70

Ha___
  William, 121
Hail
  Isaak, 77
  John, 43, 136, 137
Hailes
  Josiah, 96
Hamble
  James, 102
Hambleton
  Geo., 48, 49
Hamner
  Richardson, 143
Hampton
  Henry, 128, 131, 134
Haney
  Anthony, 109
Hannah
  John, 9, 21, 29, 30
Hardeman
  John, 68, 70
Hardin
  John, 34, 96, 100, 113
Hardman
  Charles, 23, 78, 88, 89
  William, 133, 134, 136, 137
Harris
  John, 30
  Saml., 144
  Timothy, 140
  West, 74
Harrison
  Edwd., 31
Harriss, 125
Hart
  James, 30, 75
Hartsfield
  Godfrey, 78
  Henry, 88, 144
  John, 144

Ricd., 58
Rich, 43
Richard, 42, 60
William, 88, 144
Harvey
Richard, 18
Harvie
Richard, 22, 23, 77
W., 101
William, 62, 101, 143
Wm., 34
Hatcher
Josiah, 23, 137
Haughton
James, 24
Hawk
Andrew, 28, 29, 30, 31, 32, 47, 48
Peter, 47, 136
Hawkins
Abemelick, 81
Ahemalick, 71
John, 135, 137, 139
Nicholas, 143
Hay, 47
Charles, 4, 5, 16, 103, 114, 117,
120, 123, 124, 125, 129
Gilbert, 103, 114
James, 103, 114, 135, 143
Jas., 117, 120
W., 41, 42, 43, 45, 46, 52, 59, 81
William, 47, 103, 114
Wm., 51, 54, 55, 70
Haynes
Henry, 42, 71, 73, 89
John, 42, 43
Permenus, 77, 87, 94, 99, 105,
108, 117
Phelps, 133
Richard, 117, 120, 128

Robert, 19, 62, 63, 87, 99, 117,
129
Robt., 120
Hayns
Henry, 34, 38, 39
Henderson
Robert, 23
Hendon
Isam, 77
Thomas, 62, 96
Thos., 100, 113
William, 77, 87, 99
Hendrick
Absolum, 111, 112
Henry
Anthony, 96
Elizabeth, 96
Herd
Stephen, 76
Herring
David, 34, 144
David, Jr., 144
Jno., 14
John, 4, 7, 13, 14, 18, 43, 45
Hickcock
William, 100
Higumbottom
O., 117
Hilhouse
David, 28, 39
Hill, 53
Abram, 132, 135, 146
Henry, 15, 18, 22, 46, 125, 134,
140, 143
John, 4
Miles, 133, 135, 137
Noah, 77, 86, 117
Theo, 146
Theophiles, 96
Theos., 43

Thomas, 7, 8, 21, 22, 23, 33, 37,
   42
Thos., 18
William, 33
Hillhouse
David, 9
Hinens
James, 110
Hines, 81
Elias, 46, 51, 57
James, 39, 62, 68, 105
John, 10, 13, 18, 38, 39, 55, 66,
   137
Hinis
James, 96
Hinton
Jacob, 133, 134, 136, 137
Hitchcock
James, 139
William, 96
Wm., 113
Hodge
Arch, 43, 45
George, 133
Isaac, 86, 87, 92, 117, 120
Jacob, 133
William, 43
Hodges
James, 4
Holaway
Jno., 47, 49
John, 43
Holeman
Isaac, 114, 120
Holland
Thomas, 32, 117, 120
Hollaway
John, 45, 57
Saml., 43
Holliway

John, 58
Holloway
John, 4, 7, 13, 14, 16, 18, 20, 59
Holmes
Robert, 117
Holt, 73
Harmon, 100, 144
Ratsford, 71
Hoof
Peter, 104, 137, 139
Hopper
John, 64, 77, 80
Hopson
N., 66, 67
Nicholas, 62, 63, 65, 71, 96
Horton
James, 77
Joseph, 63
House
Burwell, 133
Howell
Nathan, 43
Hubard
Joseph, 117
Hubbard
Bennett, 132
John, 43, 54, 57, 126
Jos., 120
Joseph, 123, 124, 125, 129
Hudging
John, 18
Hudspeth
Geo., 117
George, 120, 126
Thomas, 50
Hughs, 125
Thomas, 133
William, 140
Hukally
James, 63

Hunt
  James, 133, 134
Hunter
  Elisha, 33, 42, 65
Huntington
  Joseph, 26
Hurd
  Stephen, 135
Hurt
  Joel, 4, 5, 16, 34, 37, 38, 56, 63
Irvin
  Christopher, 75, 90
Jackson
  Daniel, 117, 128
  Danl., 120
  Ephraim, 105
  John, 23, 43, 45, 47, 50, 53, 144
  Wm., 117
James
  Abner, 23, 24, 59
  Joseph, 77
  Wm., 4
Jarrett
  Howell, 125
Jennens
  Robert, 43
Jennings
  Joshua, 32, 120, 128
  William, 43, 129
  Wm., 120
Jinings
  Joshua, 117
Jinkins
  E. Booker, 134
  Edm. B., 134
Jinning
  Miles, 98
Jinnings
  Levie, 145
  Robert, 44

Solomon, 96
William, 117
Wm., 57
Johnson
  Aaron, 64, 66
  Allen, 140
  Aron, 117
  Hen., 62
  Henry, 64, 66, 69, 72, 76, 78, 79,
    86
  John, 96, 133
  Luke, 144
  Miner, 88
  Nathan, 23
  Nic., 142
  Nicholas, 128, 133, 135, 140,
    142, 143, 145
  Thomas, 17, 53, 63, 76, 77, 87, 99
  William, 43, 44, 49, 50, 68, 70,
    72, 74, 78, 80, 121, 126
  Wm., 47, 57, 96, 105, 110
Johnston
  Aron, 62
Jones, 32, 33, 127
  L., 6
  Russe, 31
  Russel, 26, 31
  Russell, 11, 19
  Thos., 22
  William, 23, 49, 55, 144
Jordan
  Josiah, 33, 38, 40, 122
Jorden
  Fleming, 132
  Josiah, 42
Jordin
  Reubin, 132
Jordon
  Alaxander, 138
  Josiah, 136, 138, 143

Josey
  Henry, 6, 32
Josse
  Henry, 39
Joyce
  Alaxander, 103, 114
Kadenhead
  James, 144
Kane
  John, 63
Keaney
  James, 45
Keen
  Gilbert, 144
Kelough
  Allen, 92
  Isaac, 77
  John, 62
Kenebrew
  Laurence, 93, 99
  Shadrick, 99
Kennebrew
  Laurence, 92, 93
  Shadrack, 6
  Shadrick, 28, 93, 137
Kenney, 46, 76
  James, 28, 33, 39, 43, 46, 50, 53,
    54, 55, 56, 58, 59, 92, 93
  Jas., 45
  John, 54
  Robert, 54, 108
Kenny
  James, 9, 10, 47, 53
Kidd
  Jeames, 144
  Jno., 105
  John, 96
King
  John, 24, 25
Kinney

James, 58
Knox
  Absolum, 92
  Samuel, 92
Lacy
  Jesse, 33
Laffity
  John, 43
Lain
  Charles, 4
  Jesse, 31
Laine
  Charles, 21
  Jesse, 11
Lamar
  Elihu, 26
Lane
  Charles, 18
Langham
  William, 30
  Wm., 34
Larance
  Zac, 72
Larrance
  Jacob, 62
  Zaccariah, 62
Lasley
  William, 62
Lawrance
  Jacob, 64
  William, 23
  Zach, 64
Lawrence
  Jacob, 70
  Zaccariah, 69
Ledbetter
  Buckn., 4, 18
  Buckner, 13, 14, 16
Lee
  Greenbury, 108, 116

162

Jesse, 34, 38, 39
Jessee, 63, 133, 135, 137, 139
Jiles, 33
Seamour, 120
Semour, 117, 128
Seymour, 129
Thomas, 96
Leftridge
John, 62
Leftwich
John, 123
Leget
John, 38, 39
Legett
John, 72, 144
Legit
Jno., 104
John, 71
Letwich
John, 75
Lindsay
John, 32
Lindsey
David, 133
John, 42, 56
Lipham, 5
Little
John, 144
Lorance
Jacob, 66, 72, 79, 135, 137, 139
Wm., 117
Loveall
Solomon, 9
Low
Josiah, 117
Loyd
Ann, 138
Danl., 19, 22
Thomas, 12, 20, 43, 60, 134, 136, 137, 138

Thomas, Jr., 117
Thomas, Sr., 133
Thos., 58
Luckey
John, 96
Luckie
Hezekiah, 144
James, 143
John, 18, 22, 33, 100, 117, 120, 129
Lumberton
John, 96
Lumkin
John, 37, 38
Lumpkin, 145
Geo., 103
George, 7, 114, 121
Haroson, 106
Harrason, 72
Harroson, 71
Jno., 34, 40, 87, 90, 91, 94, 95, 99, 100, 101, 102, 103, 104, 110, 111, 112, 120, 132, 134, 137, 139, 141
John, 4, 5, 7, 8, 9, 10, 11, 12, 14, 16, 62, 86, 96, 106, 111, 112
John, Jr., 111
Joseph, Jr., 144
Joseph, Sr., 132
Pitman, 143
Robert, 10, 71, 73, 106, 127, 132, 145
Robt., 132
Lunsford
Wm., 117, 120
M___
John, 125
Macbee
James, 72
Macby

James, 71
Magbee
  James, 80, 87, 88
Mageehee
  Micajah, 62
Magnon
  James, 63
Maleir
  Richard, 75
Malone
  John, 39
Manor
  John, 5
Marbry
  James, 69
Markes
  John, 4
Marks
  James, 23, 42, 117
  John, 5, 16, 77, 87, 99
  John H., 144
Marrain
  John, 75
Martin, 112
  Barton, 34
  John, 11, 27, 144
  Joseph, 62
  Joshua, 62, 63, 135, 143
Mathews, 33
  Geo., 62
  George, 110
  George, Jr., 110
  James, 107
  Jno., 69
  John, 42, 131
  William, 33, 37, 38, 96, 106, 113
  Wm., 40, 100, 106, 107, 108
Matthews
  J., 17
  Jno., 5, 17

John, 24
Maxey
  Walter, 97, 105, 111
Maxfield
  Robert, 88
Maxwell
  Thomas, 43
McAlpin, 121
  R., 107
  Robert, 114
  Thomas, 75, 76
McBride
  William, 126
McCall
  Hugh, 4
McCammon
  James, 33, 68
McCarter
  James, 78
McCartney
  Charles, 77
  Daniel, 68
  Hannah, 68
McCaurmon
  James, 44
McClane
  John, 96
McCone
  James, 23
  Thomas, 30
McCord
  David, 48, 49, 68
  John, 34
  Robert, 5, 16
  Robt., 4
McCoy
  Edward, 123
  James, 67
McCree
  Alexr., 33

William, 33, 96, 100
Wm., 113
McCrie
William, 68
Wm., 68
Mccune
Alaxander, 89
McCune
Alaxander, 112
McCutchin
Joseph, 122
McDannel
Charles, 43
McDonald
Charles, 139
McDowell
John, 10, 28
Mcelrory
Mary, 110
McElrory
Aventon, 48
Billey, 48
Henry, 46
Jacob, 110
John, 88
Joseph, 106, 109, 110
Lewis, 106, 110
Mary, 110
Reubin, 43
William, 77, 88
McElroy
Aventon, 48
Avington, 72, 74
Billey, 48
Isaac, 77
Lewis, 109
William, 133
Willm., 38
Wm., 40
McFall

George, 9, 23
McGeehe
James, 34
McGehee
Micajah, 18, 22
McGhee
James, 144
Micajah, 143, 145
McGibberney
William, 63
McGuire
John, 97
McIntosh
Abel, 133
Daniel, 117
Danl., 4
David, 62
Jessee, 96
McLean
Saml., 144
McNab
Andrew, 18
McNalley
David, 34
McWherter
Jno., 40
John, 38, 57
Meareweather
Thomas, 133
Meariweather
Thos., 58
Mereweather
Francis, 96
Thomas, 58
Meritt
William, 34
Meriweather
Frans., 42
Thos., 43
Meriwether

Thomas, 18, 22
Merrett
  William, 44
  Wm., 44
Merrit
  William, 124
Merritt, 73
  William, 34, 64, 73
Merriweather
  Thomas, 42
Michael, 7, 25, 65, 88, 138
  John, 65, 88, 138
Milear
  Richard, 123
Miles
  Abram, 117
Miligan
  Moses, 4
Miller
  Phenias, 26
  Phineas, 8
Milner
  Jno., 60
  John, 42, 43, 58
Mitchell, 120, 123, 126, 127
  D. B., 86, 123, 126, 127, 132
Moodey
  Thomas, 43, 87
Moody
  Thomas, 34, 45, 53, 129, 132,
    135, 140, 146
Moore, 5, 41
  Edward, 73
  James, 79
  Jno., 31, 87, 113, 137
  John, 41, 45, 77, 94, 99, 100, 101,
    125, 134, 141, 143
  Michael, 133
  Saml., 57, 72
  Samuel, 54

William, 5, 24
Morgin
  John, 63
  Thomas, 77, 86, 87, 88
  William, 62
Morrowson
  Alax, 62
Morton
  Joseph, 143
Moss
  Alaxander, 142
  Nathaniel, 142, 144
  Samuel, 142
Mourton
  Joseph, 33, 37, 38, 40
Muire
  William, 4, 24
Murphey
  James, 20, 56
Murphy, 20
  James, 11, 12, 20
  Jas., 11
Musgrove, 41
  Harrason, 92, 131
  Harrison, 23, 40, 41, 68, 131
  Jane, 131
Nailer
  Geo., 50
  George, 51
Nall
  John, 16, 18, 23, 37
  Martin, 6, 28, 47
  Nathan, 4, 6, 28, 131
Nelloms
  Thos., 117
Nelms
  Thomas, 23, 37
  Thomas, Sr., 22
Newson
  Holeday, 77

Nichols
  John, 33
Noals
  Benj., 117
Noleman
  Anthony, 144
Noris
  Needham, 43
Norris
  Archer, 45, 73, 80, 117
  Hardy, 45, 80, 117
  Nedham, 53
  William, 45, 80, 133
  Wm., 45
Northan
  John, 144
Northington
  James, 4, 16, 68, 143
  Jas., 5
  Saml., 96
Norton
  Thomas, 19, 78
Ollive
  Anthoney, 62, 63
Oneal
  Nathan, 19, 22
Orr
  Christopher, 69, 74, 91
Owen
  Glen, 96, 131
  Glenn, 113
  Obediah, 55
Own
  Glen, 100
Owns
  Obediah, 54
Pace
  William, 43, 58, 60
Park, 30
  James, 19, 22

John, 30
Parks
  Ann, 109
  Aron, 109
  James, 42, 43, 58, 60, 65, 117
  John, 31, 38, 40, 42, 47, 138, 143
  John B., 122
  Joseph, 23, 37, 77
Pate
  Cordy, 23, 68
Patrack
  Paul, 24, 25
Patrick
  David, 133
  Milican, 109
  Miligin, 94
  Paul, 62
Patton, 46, 76
  Saml., 33, 39, 46
  Samuel, 9, 34, 54, 115
  Thomas, 8
  Val, 117
Payne
  John, 62
Peacock
  Jno., 58, 60
  John, 43, 58
Peck
  John, 78
Penington
  Abel, 107, 136, 137
  Isaac, 57, 133, 134, 136, 137
  Saml., 144
Pennington
  Isaac, 39
Penworth
  William, 109
Perkins
  William, 63
Perry

Willis, 63
Peters
  Jessee, 77
  William, 133, 134, 136, 137
Phair
  Ephraim, 89, 112
Pharr
  Ephraim, 18, 43
Phillip
  Mark, 37
Phillips
  George, 143
  Levi, 4, 7, 13, 14
  Mark, 33, 38, 40
  Reubin, 23
Phiniry
  Ferdenando, 38
  Ferdinando, 39
  Ferdind., 39
  Fredinan, 39
Phinizy, 59
  Ferdinand, 128, 131, 133, 134
  Ferdonand, 135
Pickens
  Andrew, 65
Pickings
  Andrew, 65
Pickins
  Andrew, 114, 120
Ponder
  Amos, 133
  Amus, 135, 140, 142, 143, 146
  Jno., 72
  John, 63, 64, 66, 69, 80
Pope
  Archels., 4
  Archelus, 7, 13
  Archs., 16, 20
  Burrell, 22, 23
  Burrl., 32, 34, 37

Burwell, 62, 106, 132, 135, 140, 142
  Elijah, 7, 16, 19, 20, 21
  Henry, 117
  Lewis, 19, 22, 104
Porter
  John, 92, 93
  Nathaniel, 23, 37, 75
Potts
  Henry, 4, 16, 18, 20
  Stephen, 19
  Stepn., 22
  William, 5, 16, 28, 42, 43, 58, 60
  Willm., 13
  Wm., 4
Pougue, 76
  Robert, 75
Powell, 95
  Edward, 50, 57, 118, 143
  Edward, Jr., 118
  Jno., 105, 108
  John, 96, 105, 111
  Semour, 118
Price
  Daniel, 69
  James, 117
Prior
  Allen, 117
  Edward, 77, 86, 88, 89, 126
  John, 62, 127
Pye
  James, 145
  Jessee, 54, 71, 78
Rachford
  Joseph, 92, 100
Radford
  Henry, 34
  Reubin, 34, 38, 39, 77
Raffety
  Richd., 37

Raffity
  Richard, 22
  Richd., 23
Ragan
  Mark, 72
Raggin
  Mark, 70
Ragsdale
  William, 70, 90, 95
  Wm., 95
Ragsdell
  Wm., 105
Raine
  John, 19, 22
Raines
  Mathew, 62, 63
Rakestraw, 18
  John, 18, 25
Ralston
  John, 141
Ramsey
  Archebel, 133
  Henry, 34, 39
  Isaac, 38
  John, 78, 87, 99
  Randolph, 27, 38
  William, 78
  Wm., 4, 117
Ratchford
  Joseph, 100
Ratsford, 73
Ray
  David, 96
  John, 11, 24
  Moses, 78
  Phil, 38
  Phillip, 33, 37, 40
  William, 43
Rayston
  Richard, 26

Read
  Alaxander, 62
  Henry, 53
  Isaak, 63
  Saml., 75
Reaves
  Malaciah, 54
  Mallachi, 55
Reed
  Collen, 13, 23
Reid
  Heny., 33
Renfrow
  William, 77
Reynolds
  John, 7, 25
  Richard, 62
  Spencer, 101, 136, 140, 141
  Thos., 19, 22
Rich
  Charles, 43, 45
Richards
  William, 133
  Wm., 4
Richardson
  Willis, 7
  Wm., 13
Richerson
  John, 62
  William, 134
Riggan
  Mark, 79
Riggin
  Mark, 64, 66
Right
  Micael, 45
Rign
  Mical, 63
Riley
  Edward, 23, 24, 29

Roan
  Hugh, 4, 7, 12, 14, 20
Robert
  Daniel, 81
Roberts
  Daniel, 42, 71, 81
Rodgers
  Joseph, 96
Roe
  Richard, 53
  Richd., 29
Rogers
  Joseph, 105, 110
  William, 8, 9, 71
Roussaux
  John, 144
Royston
  Richard, 10
Russel
  Jeremiah, 27
Russell
  Robert, 43
Rutledge
  James, 59, 77, 87, 99, 117, 120,
    129
  John, 96
  Thomas, 79
Rutlidge
  Jas., 4
Ryan
  Nathan, 4
S__
  John, 132
Saffold
  Daniel, 22
  Danl., 19
Salmon, 101
Sanders
  Britain, 66
  Britton, 62, 69, 72

James, 19, 62
James, Jr., 144
Jas., 22
Jesse, 128
Jessee, 131, 134
Sankey
  John, 42, 96, 113
  John T., 131
Sansom
  Jacob, 117
Say
  James, 128
Scoggin
  Chatt., 57
  Chatten, 133
  Phillip, 19, 22
  Thomas, 77, 99
Scoggons
  Challon, 4
Scott
  Joseph, 18, 22
  William, 18, 22
Scroggin
  Chatten, 71
  George, 34
Sellers
  John, 44, 48, 54, 57
Severson
  Nathan, 62
Shannon
  Saml., 43, 48, 53
Shanon
  Saml., 49
Sharp, 15
  John, 9, 12, 13, 14
  William, 23, 43, 96, 100
  Wm., 113
Sheapherd
  James, 45
Shepperd

170

James, 31
Shields
  John, 4, 5, 16
  Joseph, 117, 120
  Patrick, 34, 38, 39
  Thos., 117
  William, 144
Shorter
  James, 74
Shropshire, 20, 44
  J., 30
  Jno., 40
  John, 5, 23, 24, 25, 29, 31, 38, 54,
    67, 68, 89, 107
  William, 12, 20
  Winkfield, 62, 68
  Wm., 11
Simmons
  Adam, 33, 76
  Addam, 75, 114
  Addon, 113
  Asa, 18, 22, 30
Simms
  Joel, 43
Simons
  Abraham, 7
Simonton
  Adam, 30
  Margt., 30
  Robt., 30
  Thomas, 28, 30, 58, 77, 96, 100,
    113
Simpson
  Robert, 144
  Thomas, 117
Sims, 7, 25, 88, 138
  Charles, 23, 65, 78
  James, 144
  Joel, 23
  Mark, 117, 120, 126

Wiley, 117, 120
Slave
  Henry, 89
Smith
  Barnard, 43, 100, 113
  Barnet, 29
  Barnett, 23, 24
  Charles, 18, 22, 43, 58, 60, 133,
    135, 146
  Elizabeth, 91
  G., 134
  Geo., 136, 137, 138
  George, 34, 38, 39, 133, 136, 137
  Guy, 77, 96, 100, 113
  James, 43, 143
  John, 15, 43, 46, 51, 57, 60, 74,
    93, 99, 143, 144
  Peter, 117, 120, 128, 135
  Richard, 32, 33, 34, 53, 65, 92,
    100, 107, 114, 120, 121
  Robert, 51
  Saml., 62
  Samuel, 18, 22, 57, 91
  U., 78
  William, 51, 62, 63, 126, 132,
    135, 140, 142, 143, 146
  Wm., 57
Solomon
  Hezekiah, 136
Sorrel
  George, 52
Sorrow
  Henry, 78, 86
  John, 23, 24, 29, 77, 80, 86
  William, 34, 38
Sorrows
  William, 128
Spondall
  Simpleton, 9
Spurlock

Allen, 46
James, 133
Stallings, 80
James, 45, 73
Stampts
James, 144
Standaford
Benja., 38, 39
Standerpe
Shelton, 96
Standiford
Benja., 34
Starkey
John, 96
Starky
Jesse, 4, 7, 13, 14, 16, 20
Staton
Benj., 78
Benjamin, 86, 88
Jos., 22
Joseph, 19, 44, 59
William, 144
Stephens, 86, 87, 91, 95, 97, 98
Joshua, 144
Thomas, Jr., 144
W., 87, 94, 97
William, 86, 92, 94, 133
Wm., 91, 95
Stewart
Charles, 128, 144
Jno., 60, 135
John, 30, 34, 42, 43, 46, 48, 49,
50, 55, 69, 132, 140, 141, 142,
143, 145
William, 62, 63, 117
Stiles
Agness, 50
John, 8, 21, 50, 63, 66, 79
William, 32, 33, 34, 65, 107, 114,
121

Wm., 120
Stith, 4, 6, 13, 16, 19, 22, 37, 38
W., Jr., 4, 6, 13, 16, 19, 22, 23, 37,
41
Stoakes
William M., 135
Stokes
W. Muntford, 129
William M., 100
Wm. M., 113
Stone
Mathew, 48, 49
Warren, 62, 63
Stovall
Benj., 96
James, 43, 68, 102, 137
Strawther
William, 42, 43, 58, 60
Streetman
William, 23, 37
Wm., 23
Stringfellow
Benj., 115
Benjamin, 63, 122
Hen, 96
Strong
John, 135
Johnson, 123
Saml., 87
Samuel, 77, 87, 133
William, 62, 63, 96, 100
Wm., 113
Strother
William, 15, 75, 101, 140, 141
Stubblefield
Seth, 23, 29
Swain
George, 23, 37, 77
Swan
Charity, 91

Charrity, 91
Thomas, 4, 16, 18, 20
Talbot
Mathew, 68
Taliaferro, 41, 42, 43, 45, 52, 57, 63,
    66, 78
Ben, 42, 45, 52, 57, 65, 69, 74, 78,
    80
Benjamin, 62, 86
Taliafferro
Ben, 63
Tanner
Archebel, 133, 134
Archer, 136, 137
John, 88
Tarver
John, 43, 47, 48, 50, 54, 55, 57
Tate
Saml., 29
Samuel, 23, 24
Wm., 19, 22
Tatom
Eps, 28
Tatum, 90
Epps, 49, 63, 89
Eps, 34, 38, 39, 55, 62, 63
H., 91
Howel, 34, 37, 38, 40
Howell, 70, 77, 86, 89, 90, 95,
    110, 111, 115, 122
Peter, 70
Taylor
Benj., 42
Edmond, 26, 28, 39
Geo., 7, 8, 14, 15, 16, 20
George, 4, 7, 8, 14, 16, 20
Grant, 64
James, 43, 88, 90, 92
John, 133, 136, 137
Robert, 62, 64

Woody, 71, 72
Terrill
David, 68
Terry
Thomas, 18, 25, 50, 56
Thomas
Benj., 4, 7, 14, 18
Benjn., 13, 14, 16
James, 87, 89, 90, 94, 99, 110,
    127, 135, 143, 146
John, 77, 133
Joseph, 18, 22
Spencer, 4
Thompkin
Humphrey, 18
Thompkins
Giles, 63, 132
Hum., 132
Humphrey, 22, 132
Thompson
Alax, 117
Alex, 120, 128
James, 14, 20, 126, 129, 133
Jas., 4, 13, 14, 16, 18, 120
William, 27, 58, 133
Thomson
James, 78
Jas., 117
Jessee, 115
Robert, 100
Thornton
Dread, 62, 66, 72, 134, 139
Elizabeth, 103, 114
Herrod, Sr., 133
Hrad, 134
Joshua, 103, 114, 136
Noal, 120
Noel, 72, 74, 78, 80, 117, 123,
    124, 125, 129
Presley, 4, 5, 16, 28, 78, 140

Redmond, 115
Richard, 71, 92, 117, 120
Rush, 88
Thomas, 42
Thurman
David, 4
Thurmon
John, 31
Thurmond
John, 77
Thweat
James, 43
Tillery
John, 43
Joshua, 47, 49
Tompkins
Humphrey, 22, 37
Humpy., 23
Towns
John, 68, 92
Traylor
Pascal, 45, 47, 50
Pascel, 46
Paschal, 43
Pasl., 46
Travis C., 75
William, 50
Trent, 30
Henry, 27, 30, 31
Tribble
Benj., 4
Trible
Benj., 16
Benjn., 13, 14
Tuggle
Robert, 96
Thomas, 33
Tugle
Thomas, 62
Tyler

Henry, 134
Upshaw
Adkins, 50
Forrester, 50, 57, 79
Leroy, 71, 78, 79
Parsons, 50
Pasons, 79
Passons, 56, 79
Van Allen, 129
Varner
Geo., 47
George, 88, 99
Vere
William, 63
Vickars
John, 34
Vickers
John, 43
Wagnan
___, 133
Wakefield
Jno., 4
Walker, 138
R., 76
Robert, 102
William, 17, 18, 22, 43, 60, 63,
94, 100, 115, 124, 125, 143
Wm., 113, 117, 120, 123
Walters, 146
Walton, 23, 27, 47
Geo., 27, 35, 36
J. L., 76
Jno., 41, 101
John C., 25, 26
Newal, 54
Newel, 55
Ward
Richard, 117
Warnack
Robert, 9, 21

Warters
  Ann, 91
  Bradford, 117
  Joseph, 91
  Nancy, 90, 91
  William, 91
Waters
  Bradford, 120, 128
  Celia, 8
  Joseph, 129, 144
Watkins
  Benja., 34
  Moses, 117
Watson
  Douglas, 103, 114, 116, 136
Watts
  Bennet, 123
  Jacobus, 78
  John, 115
  Susannah, 123
  Thomas, 42, 98
Weaver, 96
  David, 43, 45, 87, 109
Whatley
  Mical, 62
  Michael, 66, 73
  Osnan, 77, 87, 99
  Osnon, 133
  Walton, 51
Wheelright
  Joseph, 4, 8, 10
Wheelwright, 24
  Joseph, 24, 26
White
  Moses, 34
Whitehead
  Saml., 79, 126
Whitlock
  Josiah, 133
Wilcox

Major, 102
Wiley
  Mathew, 88
Wilkerson
  Sherwood, 62, 133
Wilkes
  John, 23
Wilkins
  John, 33
Wilks
  Amos, 106
  Benj., 133, 142, 143
  Benjamin, 102, 135, 140, 145
  Jessee, 67, 80
  John, 37, 67, 88, 102, 104, 105,
    115, 116
Williams
  Aaron, 117
  Aventon, 128
  Averton, 120
  Avt., 117
  Browning, 52
  Frances, 52
  Geo., 54
  Isaac, 49, 77, 144
  Isham, 18
  Jinsey, 68
  John, 52, 77, 104
  Joseph, 52
  Morgan, 52
  Morgin, 52
  Moses, 117
  Sarah, 52
  Tabitha, 52
Williamson
  Geo., 57
  John, 10, 102
  M., 70
  Micajah, 16, 66, 69
  Samuel, 139

Stephen, 44
Willingham
  Jesse, 62, 69, 102
  Jessee, 64, 66, 70, 72, 74, 79, 80,
    102
Willis
  Nathaniel, 107
Wilson
  James, 19
  Jno., 140
  John, 28
  Jos., 68, 104
  Joseph, 5, 6, 10, 18, 32, 37, 39,
    41, 69, 74, 91, 102, 104, 106,
    139, 144
  Saml., 6, 39
  Zac, 71, 72, 96, 105
  Zach, 111
  Zacheas, 68
Wimpey
  William, 127
Wingfield
  Nathan, 96
Wise
  Joseph, 133
  Patton, 11, 121, 122, 126
Woodall
  Joseph, 19, 22

Michael, 134
Woodroff
  Clifton, 87
Woodroof
  Clifton, 77, 99
Wooten
  Job, 145
Wooton
  Jeremiah, 77, 89
  John, 86
Worrell
  Wm., 19, 22
Wray
  John, 127, 133
  Phillip, 133
Wright
  Michael, 43, 47, 50, 53
  Richd., 4
Yancey
  William, 78
Young
  John, 133
  Leo, 117, 122
  Leonard, 23, 24, 29, 120, 135
  Robert, 133
Zuber
  Abra, 43, 53
  Abraham, 19, 22, 47, 50

www.ingramcontent.com/pod-product-compliance
Lightning Source LLC
Chambersburg PA
CBHW021828020426
42334CB00014B/530